Timeless Dance

A STORY OF CHANGE AND LOSS

Timeless Dance

A STORY OF CHANGE AND LOSS

KAREN SHIFFMAN LATEINER

Timeless Dance

©2018 Karen Shiffman Lateiner

ISBN 13: 978-1717437945
ISBN: 10: 171743794X (paperback)
Paperback edition June 2018
Available in e-book

Library of Congress Control Number: 2018906457

Published by LateInks
Phoenix, AZ
ATimelessDance@gmail.com

Cover photo by Margaret Oliver

To Roger and Sarah, and to Jenni, whose spirit is eternal.

Is it possible that something as simple as taking a moment out of a busy day to smile and reflect on that moment can make the world a better place?

—*Jennifer Lateiner, 1998*

Table of Contents

An End and a Beginning

June 4, 1998. The phone rang. It was almost midnight.

This is the medical examiner's office. Are you the mother of Jennifer Lateiner?

The female voice on the other end of the line was flat, devoid of emotion. Maybe she asked if I knew Jennifer Lateiner. It's hard to remember every detail, yet bits of that conversation are branded onto my memory.

Yes. What happened? I replied, bracing myself for terrible news.

There was an accident. The worst has happened.

Her words were incomprehensible. They made no sense.

Is she alive? How is she? I blurted out.

The caller seemed annoyed as she repeated herself, this time emphatically. The tone of her voice was harsh, impatient, and abrupt.

No. This is the medical examiner. The worst has happened.

* * * * *

Jennifer was twenty-four years old when she died on a California highway near Palo Alto in the late afternoon on that fourth day of June, less than two years before the start of the twenty-first century, an event she was enthusiastic to witness. She was driving a Miata convertible sports car, the first car she bought on her own. I imagine her smile as the wind blew through her hair. Apparently, she drifted across three lanes of traffic. Her little sports car hit the divider, flipped through the air, and skidded upside down onto the pavement. She was alone. No other vehicles were involved. Her death came swiftly as help, which arrived within minutes, was too late to save her. Many hours passed before we, her parents, at home across the continent in New Jersey, were notified.

Less than two years prior to the call that shattered the silence of an otherwise ordinary night, my son Joshua revealed a life-long discomfort with his gender, something he had never before revealed. With her chosen name, Jennifer, or Jenni, for short, she was finally living as the woman she was meant to be, and we rejoiced in her happiness. Her death, sudden, senseless, and far too soon forced me to ponder life, past and present.

The grief I felt as a mother losing her son, and later the daughter she had become, was overwhelming beyond words. Yet I am compelled to share my personal story and what I learned along the way about loss and gender variance with anyone, child or adult, especially those who do not fit society's norms. Jenni's transition, at a time when it was more common for people who are transgender to hide their identities behind a façade of what was perceived to be acceptable, challenged me to understand gender in ways I had never imagined. To maintain a relationship with our children, we must get to know them as adults. Getting to know your son as a daughter is different, very different.

* * * * *

It's been ten years since the phone rang in the middle of the night. Those words echoed as fresh as the day they were uttered until I put them to paper to start writing about my journey as the mother of a remarkable human being lost to this world far too soon. I imagined the same relentless echo keeping time - fifteen, twenty, thirty years hence – until the day I die. It is now nearly twenty years, yet for me that night is frozen in time, a snapshot of the end of our lives as we knew them.

My father was a writer, a journalist, copy editor, and terrific headline writer. My sister Nita and I used to joke about giving him a ten-page paper to correct, only to have it returned as a paragraph with a great headline, succinctly answering the important questions – *Who? What? Where? When? Why?* I became an inhibited writer, one who never kept a personal journal to document thoughts and feelings, but as an older adult I learned to let my pen bypass my overly critical brain and write freely without constraints. I considered much of what I wrote to be mere ramblings, yet some may provide a glimpse into the workings of this mother's mind grappling to understand life, change, and death. Some of those writings are interspersed throughout the following pages.

* * * * *

The stark reality of death permeates existence. No matter when or how it comes, it creeps into every pore of those left alive, forever changing their lives, forever changing how they view the world, and how they act in the world. The moment of death overshadows all that came before – profoundly changing all that will come after. Prescribed stages of grief and mourning fill the spaces after that moment, but the aftermath of death remains – forever.

—KSL, May 27, 1998

I do not know why I wrote about death that particular week in May during a creative writing workshop, a week before that awful call. At the time, I was two months into the sixth decade of my life, reflecting on the past fifty years. I believe it was the impact of death in general I pondered that evening, not my own demise. Death is inevitable, no matter what one does to avoid it. Sometimes it comes without warning, or preparation, a truth I came to understand early in life.

My husband Roger, and Jenni's younger sister Sarah, are intrinsic to this story. Nonetheless, I cannot speak for them. The journey for each of us was unique and they have their own stories to tell, each from their own perspective. Mine is in the context of growing up in the mid-nineteen fifties, the child of first generation Americans, an educational psychologist, a wife, and mother. I can never fully comprehend what this experience was for Roger, as a father, to have lost a daughter, who was once his son. Nor can I understand the impact of losing a sister, who was once a brother, the person who should have been Sarah's best friend throughout her entire life. Instead, I can do nothing more than conjecture, from what I observed, what they shared, and what I surmised.

Whether together or apart, we each in our own way tried to understand what was happening as the person we had known as a precocious little boy and charming young man transformed into a beautiful woman, and what happened in a flash to change our lives in ways we could never have imagined. For those of us who knew and loved Joshua, and the few who met Jenni, our hopes and expectations for a future with her in our lives vanished the day the phone rang in the middle of the night.

Despite the proliferation of information about gender diversity since the mid-nineties when Jenni came out to us, far too many gay, lesbian, and transgender people have felt the sting of rejection by their families and by society, in addition to being actively discriminated against as a matter of religious or legislative policy. If the story of my personal journey as a mother meeting the challenge of understanding the gender transition of her child and grappling with the stark reality of her death resonates on a personal or professional level, if it starts a dialog leading to insights in the processes of acceptance and grief, or if the story of Jenni's remarkable life inspires just one person to explore the boundaries of knowledge, or to be who they truly are, I will consider my efforts worthwhile.

Jenni understood that her male personae could never be erased from our memories. In telling her story, depending on the point in time, I refer to my child as *he*, Joshua, the boy I raised and thought I knew best, or as *she*, Jenni, the woman I ached to know better as we grew older.

Karen Shiffman Lateiner

Chapter 1

Jennifer Esther Lateiner, Jenni

Jenni was a beautiful, energetic and, by all lights, a brilliant software developer, riding the technology wave of the 1990's. Two years prior to her death, Jenni had moved across the country from Boston, Massachusetts, to Portland, Oregon. It was there she emerged as the woman she always knew she was. She first came out to close friends, then her sister, and many months later, her parents. During a tumultuous year of transition from male to female, Jenni's relationship with his girlfriend whom he met in Boston and joined in Portland proved to be unsustainable. Shortly before Jenni's death however, their relationship evolved as a close friendship. Once Jenni established herself as a woman, she relocated to California to take a position at Netscape, where she met and fell in love with Margaret.

After living a childhood and adolescence in a biologically male body she neither wanted, nor understood, Jenni finally came to terms with her childhood expectations of developing a female body, knowing all along the body she saw in the mirror was not meant for her. She had never shared those feelings, and we had never seen any hint our son was struggling with his gender identity. Jenni denied all those disturbing feelings as being preposterous and tried desperately to make them go away, always thinking of herself as a woman, while living her life as a male named Joshua, the name we gave our child when we plainly saw he was a boy.

Jenni and I spoke frequently by phone, while Roger and Jenni mostly exchanged emails about work and life. Less than four months before her death, Jenni sent a handwritten letter to Roger.

* * * * *

February 10, 1998

Dear Dad,

Just got off the phone with you, and felt like writing. Sorry to hear mom talked you out of a Miata – but here are three thoughts 4 U:

1. Rent a convertible some weekend in the spring. Drive down to the Jersey Shore.* It will be worth it – just remember to enjoy the ride; traffic is OK if you're in a convertible.

* with mom, of course!

2. I'll let you drive when you visit, no prob!

...Sometimes as a kid I was jealous that you and Mom got to grow up in the 60s. Cool! But guess what, I am not jealous anymore. The human spirit is alive and well out here and everyone is quite happy! A bit of a renaissance — lots of creative energy! (Energies!) But this time is not a big revolution, it's a slow evolution, we co-exist, all in different ways...We live within the system and beyond its reach. We buy our autonomy - responsible and spiritual citizens living together on several planes. We build the Bay area technologies, make great art or do various other jobs, and

we share some common understanding of how to live beyond, as well.

Nice mix, I gotta say! I want to stay productive, and in touch. That's the new vibe – the renaissance. We don't burn out, we just burn bright! Living becomes a pleasure, working, learning, playing together here. We cooperate and grow slowly in numbers. We discuss common truths and uncover old knowledge, and we celebrate – because life, with all its challenges, can be met with a smile. We dance with life! This isn't really new, movements large and small, creative communities of varying forms have coalesced through history, and it continues here – each of us contributing something special to share with others. Burning man, we transcend, we play, we learn, we share, we laugh.

I'm motivated to share this with you -- I hope you enjoy. You and others like you (mom, friends, family) in a diverse variety of causes, in some way helped along the creation of this moment, and I wanted to thank you. Thank you and Mom for being great parents. Thank you and your generation for your discoveries. Ideas continue to be synthesized, ideas evolve, knowledge grows. Beautiful! Beautiful life process. Beautiful culture out here.

I'll transcribe some of what I am writing into electronic form to share with some of my friends, hope you don't mind.

Much love! It was great speaking to you earlier today. Hugs and kisses.

—Love, Jenni L

* * * * *

Less than ten days before she died, Jenni and Roger had another email exchange. It was their last written communication.

Jenni: Had a splendid weekend. Am extremely happy! Went to the doctor recently, and am working through all the necessaries... Can't complain though! We got a new loft bed to make our tiny bedroom bigger and Margaret's wrapped up the semester at school. She's done some really great ceramic pieces and is working on a website commission. God, I love her!

Anyway, life's fun — very, very fun. Don't forget the simple things, the magical moments. When you get a moment of peace to breathe in and reflect on all there is to celebrate about life, I strongly believe that feeling is it...If you can reach that peace, you know all you need to know in terms of uncovering happiness and living a great life — if you're centered, at one with yourself, and attempt to be at one with the environment, and help things unfold in (what you perceive to be) a positive direction.

That's all there is! I spend part of my day preparing for the future (so I can celebrate more in the future), and the rest of my day celebrating life-in-the-moment and the awe that comes from looking at the moment as a part of a much larger context (which forms a beautiful pattern as it stretches outward from the present in waves of probabilities concerning what has been and what will be).

I feel for me personally that by opening up completely to all possibilities (however terrible they may seem to the casual observer) allows me to become more at one with the underlying patters of life, and increases my feeling of being able to help things move in a positive direction.

I think I was raised in a way which allowed me to develop along the lines of "You will come to similar good conclusions that we have come to once given more good information..." I always felt that this was true — given enough information, I could make decisions that were at least as good as anyone else's. I also realized that I could consider more information at once than many people.

This is related to another area of my upbringing – the interpersonal relationships. The handbook that reads: "Guess what? You, like everyone else, are a human being living in human society" It says things like "you don't have to be a member of society, and you don't have to be a good member of society, but many people find it convenient to live this way. Choose as you will." And goes on to say things like "people have feelings. People are distractible. If you need attention, here's what to do...if you have too much attention, here's what to do......Here's how to relate to someone, and help them through their problems by being supportive, and helping them find their own solutions... (Why you might find it more beneficial to take a few close friends for dinner and drinks for about the same cost as going to a psychologist...why others may find it useful to go to support groups, or whatnot...)" Etc.

Even if I did not get as much interpersonal education as a child (my cerebral talents overshadowed my need to relate to people as peers), age taught me a bit about the benefits of treating people as equals – "Hey, I coulda' been you if things were different...how are things going for you, this alternative evolution of 'person?'"

I am thankful though that I did not have to unlearn religion, etc. I was brought up in a manner that lent itself to consequentialism and self-awareness. Very humanitarian. By discovering peace in life (as opposed to the idea that peace comes only after-life), I can accept the boundaries of mortality, and enjoy what I've got while I got it (with a momentary nod to the future, thus allowing me to enjoy more even after the moment passes).

Overall, I am happy to be part of the cycle – whereby eventually another generation comes into the picture to take over my activities: celebrating life and preparing for more celebrations in the future! After all, I'm probably from a long line of people who did basically the same things...celebrate life and help prepare for more to celebrate in the future.

Isn't that neat?

Another happy fabric tile in the quilt of life.

Another happy participant in the ongoing dance of life.

—Jenni

* * * * *

By all accounts – emails and phone calls, Jenni appeared to be happy, very happy with her new life, and we were grateful. It was a long journey for her to arrive at this point. It should never have ended so soon.

The last time any of us saw Jenni was in March 1998. Roger and I flew to San Francisco to celebrate my fiftieth birthday with Jenni and Margaret. Sarah, then a freshman at Oberlin College, flew in from Ohio to meet us. Despite her disappointment at not spending her first spring break with friends, and Roger's protests of being too busy to take time off from work, I insisted we all go, at the very least for a long weekend. More than anything, I wanted to celebrate my milestone birthday together as a family. I refused to back down. Reluctantly, they both agreed. Over the years since then, I have learned to respect strong impulses to call, reach out, visit, or just tell someone I am thinking of them.

Jenni and Margaret met us at the gate. They handed me a card with a picture of a baby, naked except for a black box covering the genitals, and the words, *It's a...* Inside the card simply read *A BABY*. Underneath Jenni wrote, *Happy Birthday, Mom – always keeping you on your toes!* At first, I imagined that a baby might be on the way, but my momentary fantasy of becoming a grandmother evaporated with a resounding denial. The card was a declaration that Jenni, was my child, and would always be my child, although I never doubted it for a minute. *She* was her gift to me. I think she wanted me to know, as if I didn't already, that times were changing. If only she were alive today to see just how much things have changed.

At some point after Jenni first came out to us, Roger talked to Jenni about the possibility of freezing sperm before completing her transition, should she want to parent a biologically related child in the future. We learned later, after her death, that she had made attempts, but was unsuccessful in obtaining a viable sample. Jenni even went so far as to stop taking hormones for a while, but it was already too late in the process. She would have been a wonderful mother. I'll never forget the expression on teenaged Joshua's face as he held his infant cousin for the first time. It was nurturing and sweet, not at all awkward as might be expected from an adolescent boy.

During our stay, we visited Muir Woods, a place where giant redwoods and Sequoias towered over us, blocking out of most of the bright California sky. I walked in silence, reflecting on the timelessness of the universe, appreciative of these precious moments with the people I loved most in life, including the person Jenni was planning to marry. Dinner in the Haight-Ashbury District of San Francisco topped off a perfect day. Jenni and Margaret took us to a *hookah* lounge for Middle Eastern food to celebrate my birthday and our twenty-ninth wedding anniversary.

Roger and I were married on my twenty-first birthday. After three years of struggling to make our way as college graduates in the adult world we decided on an adventure. We gave up our tiny attic apartment in Queens, New York, to travel through Europe and spend a year living on a *kibbutz* in Israel. The cuisine of the Middle East was familiar to us, but this was our first time in a *hookah* lounge. It was dark but inviting, with benches softened by patterned pillows and wall shelves festooned with ornate water pipes, each reflecting their country of origin. The sweet smoke of scented herbs filled the air.

The Haight had changed dramatically since the 1960s when it was the center of the psychedelic era. Nevertheless, it seemed to retain some of its quirkiness and charm. It was an odd mix of aging hippies, students, urban pioneers, panhandlers, homeless youth and social service workers offering help to the needy and food to the hungry. Shops filled with trinkets and memorabilia catered to nostalgic tourists.

When we left the restaurant after dinner, Jenni and Margaret, a few steps ahead of us, suddenly quickened their pace, signaling us not to linger. We hurried to keep up with them. Once safe in the car, they told us they felt frightened and vulnerable as they passed a group of people gathered on the street. They told us that lesbian couples elicited stares and hateful comments, even in this seemingly more open-minded and accepting city. The magic of a perfect day dissipated at that moment. I feared for their safety and longed for a day when no one would ever be afraid to walk down the street with the person they loved.

Jenni and I held each other in a long embrace as we said goodbye at the airport. She lamented the distance between us and wished she were able to join us to celebrate Passover that spring, as she had the year before when family and friends gathered around our table to welcome her home.

Karen Shiffman Lateiner

Chapter 2

Continuity

For me, holidays represent an opportunity, or perhaps an excuse to cook traditional foods and reflect on the history of my ancestors and the evolution of our observances. Rich in meaning and interpretation, Passover was always a favorite. In our home, the annual telling of the biblical story of Moses leading his people from bondage in Egypt to the land of Israel invariably led to discussions of modern day slavery and genocide, and the need to remain vigilant in protecting human rights for all people to remain truly free. I cannot help but wonder if as a child, listening to stories of freedom from bondage, Joshua pondered liberation from a body that did not match her identity, adding yet another dimension to the theme of the holiday. Years after her death, we learned that Jenni organized her own Passover Seder in Portland. Piecing together childhood memories, she gathered her friends for dinner and led a Seder at her home, complete with the songs we sang at our family Seders.

My earliest recollections of Passover were of formal Seders in the back of my paternal grandfather's tailor shop in Hoboken, New Jersey, where he lived with his fourth wife. *Zaide* and *Bubbe* (Yiddish for grandfather and grandmother) prepared a traditional feast for the entire family in their tiny kitchen and served it on rented tables covered in white cloths.

In 1902, *Zaide* left Russia in search of a better life in America, safe from pogroms, safe from being beaten or slaughtered because he was Jewish. He found work making raincoats in a factory in New York and soon sent for his wife and their child, Rose. His younger sister, Anna, two years older than Rose, was supposed to leave Russia with them, but at the last minute was not allowed because of a childish spat between the two girls, who had been as close as sisters. My father, Mack, was born in 1908 in New York, after his sister, Geraldine, but before his brother, John.

Zaide suffered one hardship after another beginning with the death of his first wife following a miscarriage, when John was only two years old. Luckily, a young woman, who had recently arrived in America, helped take care of my father and his siblings. They married and soon after had a daughter, Molly, followed by a son three years later. Not long after, this beloved woman succumbed to the flu epidemic and the baby boy was sent to a nursery for care, but at twenty months, he too died. Desperate to find someone to care for his children, he arranged to marry another woman who had just arrived from Russia. Many years later after her death, *Zaide* married the woman we knew only as *Bubbe.*

Through all of his struggles, *Zaide* never lost his faith. He persevered, provided for his family, and sent money to his brothers and sisters who eventually joined him in America. Throughout his life, he remained steadfast in his commitment to the traditions of his ancestors, kept a kosher home, attended synagogue, and recited the entire Passover Seder in Hebrew. Seders at my grandfather's house were very long. My cousin Harvey, the oldest cousin, brought toys to entertain me at the table, as I was the youngest. Despite a twenty-five-year age difference, we continue to enjoy a close relationship.

After the traditional feast, including prayers and songs, the younger cousins practiced sewing buttons and played hide and seek amongst the clothing hanging in the tailor shop. To this day, the scent of chicken soup with matzo balls never fails to remind me of the musty old suits hanging above those ornate sewing machines with cast iron foot pedals.

I have no memories of celebrating holidays with my maternal grandparents, although we visited often, and Grandma made the best potato *kugel,* a traditional Eastern European dish served as part of a Sabbath meal. They were immigrants from Eastern Europe but met in New York City. At the age of sixteen, accompanied by a slightly older cousin, my maternal grandmother, Anna, left her home in the eastern part of the Austro-Hungarian Empire. She tried to adapt to modern life of the times, but still insisted upon keeping a kosher home. Despite being fluent and literate in five languages, she found English spelling difficult to master and we grandchildren delighted in giving her English lessons.

My grandfather, Max, whom we called Papa just as my mother did, came from the same general area in Europe. After being blacklisted for union organizing in Brooklyn, he started his own business as a tinsmith and roofer. As many immigrants did at the time, and still do today, Papa worked hard to help bring other members of his family and his wife's family to America.

In contrast to my grandmother's insistence on keeping a kosher home, Papa was eager to redefine himself in the New World. He was far more interested in eating shellfish and pork, the forbidden foods of kosher cuisine, than practicing religion, although he maintained a strong Jewish identity. I remember sitting in the back of his black 1950 sedan for an outing to the famous Lundy's Restaurant at Sheepshead Bay in Brooklyn. It was fascinating to watch him eat clams and oysters, something none of his grandchildren dared try, until they were much older.

I loved visiting my maternal grandparents in Brooklyn, especially when we were given nickels to buy Mello-roll ice cream, a creamy delight wrapped in a paper cylinder to be carefully unwrapped after it was placed in a specially shaped wafer cone. Papa taught us to plant vegetables and Grandma kept us supplied with paper bags, bowls, and buttons to set up a pretend grocery store, complete with a strainer hung on the wall as a scale to weigh out our purchases. I still treasure my collection of buttons, some saved from childhood.

My mother, Esther, who was the oldest of their children, spoke Yiddish until she entered school, as many children of immigrants did in those days. Her sister, Tillie, was born less than a year later, followed by Nathan, and then Frank. Music was almost as important as putting food on the table in their home, and the children were enrolled in classes at the Henry Street Settlement House, which still stands today on the Lower East Side of Manhattan. My mother played piano and sang, and my aunt played the violin.

My parents chose to affiliate with a conservative synagogue, where we attended Friday night Sabbath services to hear my mother sing in the choir. To augment my public school education, I attended Hebrew School most afternoons after school. After the death of my father when I was fifteen years old, religion and rituals lost all meaning for me. I found no solace in them.

Roger's parents were also first generation children of Eastern European Jews who arrived in this country around the turn of the century. His family was less observant than mine, though in an effort to fit in with his friends, he attended Hebrew School and had a *Bar Mitzvah*. During a year in Israel living on a non-religious kibbutz, Roger and I celebrated Jewish holidays as cultural and seasonal events. For our children, we chose a secular Jewish education with an emphasis on history, literature, and culture. In our home together, we created our own traditions celebrating Passover as an opportunity to be with family and friends, connect the past to the present, explore non-traditional *Haggadahs,* and reinforce for our children the significance of freedom, social justice, and the importance of advocating for human rights throughout the world.

Jenni never told us about her Portland Seder. Perhaps she wanted to create her own tradition with her own interpretation, just as Roger and I created ours, different from those of our parents and grandparents. Whatever her motivation, I imagine she was defining her own way of doing things as an adult, an adult exercising her right to determine the direction of her life, just as her parents, grandparents, and great-grandparents had before her.

Family was important to Jenni. I know she imagined many family gatherings in the future as we all grew older and our relationships matured. When we parted at the airport, in the midst of hugs and tears, not knowing this would be the last time, we promised to always remain close and stay in touch, despite the miles separating us.

* * * * *

The call came less than three months later. Jenni and I spoke on the phone about an hour before the accident. She was preparing to leave her apartment in San Jose to drive to San Francisco to pick up a computer for her home office when I called to say hello. After being laid off by Netscape while they struggled to survive as a viable company, Jenni easily found a job as a software developer with another company. When the new company decided to relocate out of state, Jenni was given the opportunity to continue working for them from her home in California. In the midst of our conversation, Jenni said she was looking for her checkbook and proceeded to turn her search into a comedy routine. We laughed at the absurdity of things disappearing for the young and the not so young.

Do you still love me even if I can't find things? She quipped.
Do you still love me when I can't find things? I asked.
She giggled.
Don't worry, Jenni. I'll always love you. I added.
I love you too, Mom.

Those were the last words between us, the last time I heard my child's voice.

It was sunny and clear when Jenni left her home to drive to San Francisco, but it was overcast all day in New Jersey. Sarah, home from school for the summer, was living in a dorm in Manhattan, taking summer classes at New York University. She decided to come home for the weekend and had arrived earlier in the day. The three of us went out to dinner with plans to rent a movie to watch at home as we waited for a torrential downpour predicted for later in the evening.

By the time we finished dinner and walked next door to the video store, the storm arrived in full force, well ahead of schedule. We waited inside for the rain to let up before attempting to reach our car. Mesmerized by the sheer force of the downpour, I watched as cars inched their way through the flooded streets. With a sudden shudder, I imagined Jenni driving her little car in awful conditions. I was grateful Sarah was safe with us, not on the road. I wished the four of us were huddled close, protecting each other from the storm.

There are times when a mother is overcome with a feeling deep within her that her child needs her, is calling out to her, and she should be with her child. Rationalized away and shrugged off at the time, I still cannot help but wonder if my sudden desire to gather Jenni in my arms coincided with the moment in time my child needed me most, as her life slipped away.

Chapter 3

There's Always Next Time

We saw Jenni four times after she came out to us. In November 1996, we traveled to Los Angeles for Roger to attend a national meeting of the Screen Actors Guild where he worked. I joined him to attend my cousin's wedding the same weekend. We had not seen our son Joshua for nearly a year. Meeting in California was a perfect opportunity to be together. Jenni came out to us that weekend.

Months after getting past the initial shock of finding out that my son was now my daughter, Jenni agreed to meet us at a gender identity clinic in Minneapolis, where we had arranged for her to be evaluated professionally for the best course of action. Jenni came home for Passover the following spring and again for the Christmas holidays at the end of the same year. Our trip to California to celebrate my birthday in March of 1997 was the last time we saw her.

The initial period of her transition was a time of great cognitive dissonance for me. The first time I saw my son dressed in female clothing I felt as if I were peering through a kaleidoscope seeing my child at one turn a boy, at another a girl, the same pieces assembled in a different pattern. Jenni. Joshua. Jenni again. Back and forth, male, female, boy, girl, the images kept changing, as I struggled to maintain the image of the woman Jenni wanted everyone to see. Over time it became easier. A beautiful young woman, my daughter who was always there, began to emerge physically, reminding me she was still the same person, the same kind, loving person.

During her first visit home, we invited friends and family to join us for Passover, grateful that Jenni's aunts, uncles and a few family friends came to celebrate the holiday and welcome our child home with open arms and unconditional love. Some, however, refused our invitation, giving various excuses for declining to celebrate with us as we had in years past.

Not everyone was ready to see Joshua, their friend, neighbor, or cousin, as the woman she had become. It was incongruous, too much to comprehend, let alone face. Excuses for not seeing Jenni ranged from superficial to honest. No one was unkind. They just stayed away. I tried to be understanding.

It is not easy to adjust to such an unexpected change. I wanted to protect Jenni by carefully choosing encounters in the neighborhood. Even my own hesitation to go to the supermarket with Jenni, where we might run into people we knew, came as a surprise to me. If I needed something at the store, I found myself running out of the house alone on the pretense of making a quick trip. I am still not sure if I was protecting her or protecting myself from questions I was not prepared to answer. If the latter, Jenni surely saw through me, but never said anything.

At the end of the same year, December 1997, Jenni came home with her girlfriend, Margaret, who had never been to New York. We toured Manhattan to see the holiday lights and had dinner at a Greek restaurant on the Upper West Side. After our meal, Margaret turned to us and asked for Jenni's hand in marriage. What a sweet gesture to formally announce their intentions. Without hesitation, we gave our consent. At the time, same sex marriage was not legally recognized anywhere in the United Sates, but despite their outward appearance as a same sex couple, Jenni was still technically a male, and legally able to marry a woman.

We had once had the privilege of attending a wedding under similar circumstances, this time a man, born female, married another man. In performing the ceremony, the judge stood before the two men and triumphantly stated, *I now pronounce you...um...MARRIED!* It was brilliant, striking us as how it should be.

As the waiter took our dessert orders, I blurted out that our daughter had just become engaged to marry. I was excited and had to tell someone, anyone. Within minutes, he returned to our table with his manager who was carrying glasses filled with sweet liquor for a proper celebration, Mediterranean style. Hearty congratulations from guests and staff filled the room, all sharing this joyous moment with people they did not know. This was truly a New York moment. Together we toasted to life, to health, and to love, without anyone so much as raising an eyebrow at the two women at our table who were holding hands and displaying affection towards one another

Jenni and Margaret graciously declined my offer to make an engagement party while they were in town. Whether this reflected their hesitation in making a general announcement, or if they were merely not interested in a party remains a mystery. It had taken many years for Jenni to come out to herself, and it had taken some time for us to adjust to the transformation still in process. While it might have come as a shock to some that our son, now a female, was marrying a woman, it appeared totally logical to us. They were in love. Nothing else mattered. There would be a celebration the next time they came to our home. I imagined planning a wedding ceremony under a floral canopy of the giant Magnolia tree that graced our yard, with family and friends gathered to celebrate the marriage of Jenni and Margaret. There was no next time.

Karen Shiffman Lateiner

Chapter 4

Final Arrangements

The days following Jenni's death were a blur of activity. Sedatives dulled my senses and fogged my brain. We flew to California to make final arrangements parents are not supposed to make for their children. At the medical examiner's office, we confirmed Jenni's identity by her clothing and the contents of her wallet. They would not allow us to see her, and we were too much in shock to press the issue. I wished I had been able to see her hand, at the very least, to hold it one last time. I tried not to think about the damage to her beautiful body, yet it helped us in the decision to cremate, which had become a tradition in Roger's family.

The receptionist at the coroner's office was cold and abrupt, reminding me of the person who called in the middle of the night. I wondered if this lack of warmth might have been a reflection of bias towards Jenni as a transgender woman still in the process of fully transforming her body. In a more perfect world, I might have imagined at least some expression of sympathy directed towards every grieving person who had to enter this awful place, regardless of one's personal opinion or bias.

We were put in touch with a local rabbi who helped arrange a memorial service at her reformed synagogue in Los Gatos. Jenni's friends and coworkers were notified, and together with a few family members who lived close-by, we celebrated Jenni's life and mourned her death. The only hint of Jenni's prior life was the Rabbi's pronouncement of her Hebrew name, *Mordecai Jehoshua*, along with her chosen English name, Jennifer Esther, as the traditional prayer for the dead was recited. I've heard the same prayer hundreds of times in my life, the Mourner's Kaddish, always recited in the original ancient Aramaic, yet I have never been able to commit it to memory. Tears always got in the way. Those same words recited for my child sounded like a judge's gavel – it's over, ended, the decision is final. She's dead.

We had named our son Joshua Sebastian, a melodic combination based on Roger's love of whistling the Brandenburg Concertos of Johann Sebastian Bach. As is customary in Jewish families, we also gave our baby a Hebrew name, *Jehoshua*, for Joshua, and *Mordecai*, in memory of my father, reversing the two for their cadence. Never could we have imagined the names we carefully chose for our baby boy would prove to be so ill-fitting.

Jenni's friends and coworkers in California knew her only as a woman, and we felt she would have wanted to be remembered by them as the woman they knew her to be. Family members, who knew her only as Joshua, referred to her as Jenni that day out of love and respect. The few who recognized her Hebrew name as male confirmed what they may have suspected...that Jenni was a transgender woman. Nonetheless, to those gathered it did not matter. The finality of death eclipsed gender change.

For hours, we heard stories of Jenni's brilliant mind, her exuberance, and her love of life. As a software developer at Netscape, she was often seen gliding through the corridors on rollerblades, stopping at cubicles to introduce herself and make inquiries of each person's project. Her hair might be blonde, or jet black. Sometimes it was purple, or green. Always, her uncanny intelligence shined through as she asked questions and suggested solutions to problems. With an infectious smile and not a bit of shyness, Jenni made many friends. The image of her skating through the office with purple hair forced me to smile even on that dreadful day. It still does.

With great enthusiasm, as she approached everything that caught her interest, Jenni joined the planning board for *Burning Man,* a community of free spirited people who gather annually in the Nevada desert to construct temporary art installations. She was excited about participating for the first time that summer, the summer of 1998. Instead, a memorial board was erected in her name.

Upon return to our home to New Jersey, we held another memorial in our backyard, a place of celebrations and memories. A tent to shield us from the sun was put up next to the house alongside our giant Magnolia tree, where I had hoped one day to see my children marry. Instead it protected us from an unexpected downpour. The sun refused to shine that sad day.

Again, friends and family gathered – more than we expected. Those unable to fit inside the tent stood outside under umbrellas, with their shoes sinking into the rain soaked lawn. Friends, relatives, neighbors, and teachers told stories about Joshua, the boy they had known. That he grew up to be a woman was a surprise to everyone. The impression Joshua made as a child and as a teenager mirrored the one Jenni made in California – brilliant, creative, interesting, generous, and compassionate, a very sweet person with a good heart. Again, death overshadowed gender change.

* * * * *

During the nineteen seventies, eighties, and well into the nineties, before the proliferation of information on the Internet, transgender awareness was not part of the general consciousness. Discussions of gender identity and sexual orientation were absent from public school curricula, and libraries had few, if any books that even touched upon the subject Even in large cities, specialty book stores addressing gay and lesbian concerns contained very few references to transgender issues.

Before telling friends and family about Jenni's transition we had learned as much as we could, but the telling was far from complete. Many in our circle of friends and extended family learned of the transition at the same time they were informed of our child's death. We are grateful my sister and Roger's sister welcomed Jenni and spent time with her when she visited. They were the ones to break the news to our extended families, while a close family friend called other friends to inform them of Jenni's death. *Joshua, son of Karen and Roger Lateiner, known for the last two years as Jennifer Esther, Jenni for short, died in an automobile accident on June 4th, 1998* was repeated many times and questions were answered. It was a double shock to most, but again, death emerged as the worst that happened.

Jenni had chosen *Esther* as her middle name, after her beloved Grandma Esther, my mother, with whom she had a special bond. My mother died before Jenni came out to us, but I often wonder if she had an inkling of Joshua's struggle with identity. Without a frame of reference to shape any questions or concerns she might have had, she just listened as her grandson entertained her with fantastic ideas and imaginative stories. Someone suggested it was good she did not live to experience the untimely death of her grandchild. To me, it was far from good. I wished she could comfort Sarah in the magical way of grandmothers. I myself longed for her unconditional love and reassurance that life would go on as it had for her and her parents after the death of her young brother.

I remain eternally grateful for the other mothers, those nurturing women within our social networks whose presence was keenly felt. They were there when we needed them, always ready to listen and console. A local female owned bookstore, where Sarah worked after school throughout high school, set up a display of books related to lesbian, gay, and transgender issues, as well as dealing with the loss of a child. Montclair was, and still is known to be a liberal, welcoming town, yet people in our community wanted to become more educated, especially about transgender issues.

At the memorial, anticipating many questions, Roger and I stood at the podium and told stories about our child, her life as Joshua and her life as Jenni. We wished everyone had the opportunity to see for themselves the metamorphosis of our son to become the beautiful, easy-spirited woman she was meant to be, the same person we all knew and loved. Telling Jenni's story, along with the stories of others whose identity did not match their bodies enabled me to function that day and the days following, holding at bay the stark, bitter reality that I would never see my child again, hear her voice, or hold her in my arms.

Karen Shiffman Lateiner

Chapter 5

Period of Mourning

We buried Jenni's ashes in the cemetery where my parents are buried. Although it was more than a week after Jenni's death, when we returned home from California, we commenced a *Shiva* period, the customary week of withdrawing from responsibility to mourn a loved one according to Jewish tradition. It was impossible to do much else. The *Shiva* period is a time to heal and let the wound scab over, a time for the body to regain its strength for the long road ahead. After the death of a family member my ancestors observed a full year of mourning following the initial seven days of most intense mourning at home. For one year, they recited daily prayers and refrained from participating in celebrations, although they did return to work. At set times every year thereafter, anniversaries and holidays, they lit memorial candles and recited the traditional prayers for the dead. While the religious aspect held little interest to me, the therapeutic value of these ancient traditions made perfect sense.

By the end of the week, I stopped taking the sedatives my doctor had prescribed. The time had come to feel the pain and adjust to the reality of life without my child. By the end of the first year, a veil lifted as I reconciled myself to never seeing Jenni again. Instead, I made a place in my mind for her kind spirit and love of life to be with me always. Out of sequence and the natural order of life, the death of a child is life-changing. Children are supposed to outlive their parents. The absence of one's child lasts forever, no matter how many days, weeks, or months of mourning are observed, how many prayers said, or candles lit.

During those first weeks, friends, family, neighbors, and acquaintances came to share memories, listen to whatever we wanted to say, or sit silently with us when there was nothing any of us could say. Some came every day, some stayed through to the night, and others stayed overnight, so we would not be alone. We were grateful for their presence. It is an Eastern European Jewish tradition to bring sweetness to a house of darkness and tears. When my father died, our more traditional house of mourning overflowed with little more than cakes, candies, and cookies, marking the beginning of my life-long struggle to resist sweets. When Jenni died, I was grateful for the diversity of our social circle and a broader interpretation of what had been customary in earlier generations. Our friends brought us healthy meals, set our table, and joined us in the simple daily routines of mealtime, nourishing us body and soul with generosity and love.

One afternoon during the first week at home, Jim, a close family friend coaxed me outside to once again experience the world beyond my front porch where I spend many hours, either alone or with dear friends. My legs felt too heavy to move, but with encouragement, I stepped down onto the sidewalk, repeating in my head to take one step at a time, just one step at a time. It was all I could do, nothing more and nothing less.

I needed to find a new state of homeostasis, a sense of equilibrium amidst the bombardment of events determined to upset the balance of my mind and body. One step at a time, I continued my journey as a mother who lost her daughter who was once her son. Each day another opportunity to gather my experiences, integrate them into my being, and use what they taught me to face the future.

A year or so before, Jim invited Jenni for dinner while he was visiting San Francisco. It was still early in Jenni's transition and I was anxious to know how well she passed as a woman. Jim reported no trouble seeing her as a woman, but admitted he had a hard time getting past the nose ring. Although I was glad Jenni passed well, I too was not thrilled about the nose ring. If only I could have Jenni now, she could have as many nose rings as she wanted. Of course, this is easy to say - now that she is gone.

Jim's report meant a lot to me. Given the reality of intolerance and hate crimes, I feared for Jenni's safety. I worried about how others would see her. Not everyone accepts or even tolerates people who are gay, lesbian, transgender, or worse, transitioning. Upon learning of Jenni's death, one of her cousins assumed she had been murdered or beaten to death because she was a transgender woman. How sad we live in a society where such dreadful acts, committed out of hate born of ignorance are almost expected. While not the cause of Jenni's death, this is the cause of countless others, directly or indirectly. I weep for them all, and for all their mothers, fathers, and siblings.

For the memorial we put together a photo montage of our child to chronicle her life from childhood to young adulthood - boy to man, man to woman, woman in love with a woman. There were many questions about why a person might choose to change their gender to go from heterosexual male to lesbian woman. I welcomed any opportunity to explain. Most of all, I wanted to be in control of how my child would be remembered.

First, I clarified the misconception many had of gender identity and sexual orientation as a choice, rather than a physiological and psychological imperative, a powerful need to fulfill in order to proceed with one's life. With the help of pamphlets and articles I had accumulated, I explained the concept of gender identity and sexual orientation as two different aspects of being. I wanted everyone to understand and accept not just my child, but every person who does not fit the male-female, heterosexual pattern. I felt the need to talk about the variation in biology, identity, and sexual preference beyond the typical binary conceptualizations of male-female, or gay-straight.

Most of the questions were reasonable, demonstrating genuine interest in a subject heretofore not generally discussed or even contemplated. Each one illuminated the need for our society to be better informed and educated. I tried to answer to the best of my knowledge, but had to respond to one question with a query. *Do you discuss the mechanics of your adult child's sex life?*

The question was asked innocently and without malice. Yet, I felt violated, not only for myself and my child, but for every gender non-conforming person who is asked personal questions about their bodies, or their intimate life. My child deserved the dignity and respect one would give to anyone, and should give to everyone, dead or alive, regardless of whether they fit into a preconceived mold.

I recalled a conversation I had many years earlier. It was in the mid 1960s, while I was visiting my aunt and uncle—my mother's younger brother and his wife—in their home in a New England college town. One evening they discussed the sexual revolution of the times with their friends. Being somewhat naive, just beginning to test my own independence and sexuality, I was interested in hearing the views of this intellectual group gathered around the fireplace. The comment of an older gentleman, a professor no doubt, was most salient. He said that sex was but one part, a very small part, of a loving relationship. I doubt I understood it then, but now, more than ever, having been asked a question about my child's sex life, a question I never should have been asked, its meaning became crystal clear and I was able to respond. *There are many ways to have a loving relationship, and many ways to be a human being.*

There are many ways to be a human being. A friend's elderly mother said this to me after she was told about Jenni's transition. Her wise words gave me clarity shortly after my child came out, a time when I was still very confused by what was happening. When I repeated this phrase, I hoped it conveyed the idea that life, love, people, and relationships might be viewed more broadly.

During those first weeks of mourning, explaining and educating was exhausting, but it diverted my attention from the reality of Jenni's death. I could not endure grieving, yet I knew I would grieve forever. Stories about Jenni, her childhood, transitioning, our reactions, and other people's reactions kept us busy and sometimes even amused. One anecdote particularly put life squarely into perspective.

Months before, excited to announce our child's engagement, we called our friends, Jim and Adele, with the news. They congratulated us and asked which one - Jenni or Sarah?

Jenni, I replied.

Uh - What's the person's name? Adele asked.

Margaret.

Always?

Yes.

Is she Jewish? she asked next.

No.

Will that be a problem? She asked.

With that, we all burst out laughing. How, in the scheme of things, could this be important? We laughed then at the absurdities of life, and again whenever we retold the story. We imperfect humans tend to place so much importance on things that, in the end, in matters of life and death, no longer matter. Death, no matter how tragic and awful, can leave a most valuable gift to those open enough to take it - renewed appreciation of life and all its variation.

Karen Shiffman Lateiner

Chapter 6

Aftermath of Death

I drifted in a daze through the days, weeks, and months after Jenni's death. Friends and relatives came and went. Some knew what to say and do. Others awkwardly tried to console us. I often wound up consoling them. They coaxed us to join them for outings and dinners. Sometimes we agreed. Other times we could not find the strength. Roger and I clung to each other, speechless. There was nothing we could say. We went through the motions of life barely functioning, yet sometimes over-functioning to mask our grief, or at least push it aside. We held ourselves together with memories of Jenni, memories of Joshua, memories of our child. I returned to the writing workshops I had previously attended.

* * * * *

I drove to the cemetery today with a rose to place on the mound of earth covering your ashes. A red rose just like the one you gave me for my birthday. Can I ever forget your smile as you presented it? The smile you always smiled as your goodness burst out of you. And now, here I sit under the great maple tree in the cemetery. We chose this place to bury your remains. It sounds so strange to say your remains, when your remains are your spirit, the memory of you, the mark you left on everyone who knew you, and thoughts of you by those who know your life story. This is what remains of my child, so full of life, full of joy, full of happiness.

Your grave is alone – no other monuments near. Open space of grass dotted by mature trees and bushes - and then rows of stone. You lay in the shadow under a tree that changes color every autumn. My sweet child – you never sought the sun. You did not need it. Instead you carried sunshine with you, radiating it even in the dark. Did you learn to enjoy the California sun as a beautiful woman riding around in your convertible sports car? You look so happy, so free, in the photographs you sent.

Jenni – my sweet Jenni. The child I carried and raised as my son, never knowing your confusion and disappointment at not growing up to be the woman you always thought you would become. I never knew your secrets, only your smile. You were precious always – son or daughter. I lost you both – mourned twice. But I also rejoiced twice, as you would not hesitate to remind me – your birth, and then your rebirth. You left us too soon. Pieces of my heart are buried here with you. Yes, you will live on in your writings and through the memories of all you touched. But I will never see your smile again. Never share in your happiness again. I know you did not want to leave this world so soon. I hope you at least found peace.

Images of you meeting those who died before you flash through my mind. They give me some comfort, if not a smile. But I know these are mere imaginations. I'd like to think you'll meet your Grandma Esther, my mother, whose name you took as your middle name. Maybe it is true you will meet all the souls from whence you came. All the souls whose imprint you carry. There is a spot not too far from here -- at the end of the front row of stones. We were told ancient books are buried there. You loved old books, anything rare and valuable, like yourself. Grandma Esther's grave is across the little road from you, next to her husband, Mack, my father, the grandfather you never met, another kind and gentle soul, and all the line of people you never met, but whose genes you share. Perhaps you'll meet them now. You might meet Phyllis, my great aunt Anna's daughter. I never met her. I am told she too was a shining star, an adventurer, like your little sister, Sarah. Phyllis planned to go to Palestine as a pioneer, before it became the State of Israel, but died before her journey began, lost forever in her early twenties, slightly younger than you when you left us. Now I know the pain her mother carried all her life. I understand the pain of all mothers, all parents who have lost their children.

Before today, I never came here by myself – never came to visit anyone's grave. Yet I could not stop thinking about coming here today. It is almost the three- month anniversary of your death, and we are preparing to visit Margaret, the woman you loved, to go through your belongings, to review your life. It is a terrible task we have ahead, but we expect to learn more about you as we get glimpses of your life. Please be assured it will be done with utmost respect for all aspects of you. You were a complex being of ideas. You will continue to shine – you have left your mark.

But I will never see your smile again, except for the one frozen in memory the time you presented me with a rose for my birthday. It was the same beautiful smile accompanying your very first presentation of a dandelion bouquet. My sweet precious child – I will never stop loving you, or thinking about you.

—KSL, September 1998

With each passing day, Roger and I felt the need to meet other people like us, other people whose child was dead. A support group seemed to be the answer. It was an hour long drive to the first monthly meeting. Hand-printed cardboard signs posted at the back entrance of an old church led us to a basement classroom. A woman greeted us, wrote our names on name tags, smiled warmly as she held our hands, nodded her head, and softly said, *I know.* We joined the others seated in a large circle of folding chairs that filled the entire room. The leader introduced us as new members. Everyone nodded a sad, but understanding, nod. They too *knew.*

One by one, everyone in the group introduced themselves, stated the name of their child, their age at death, and how long ago it had been. Each person went on to tell their story in more detail and report on how they were coping, or not coping. The stories were heartrending – chronic or sudden illness, murder, suicide, drug overdose, drowning, car accidents...the list went on.

Parents talked about the loss of their babies, young children, teenagers, and adults. For some, it was weeks since their lives took this awful turn, shattering all their hopes and dreams. For others, it was years. For all, no matter what the circumstances of their child's death, and no matter how old their child was, it was devastating. We were surprised to hear that the pain can linger for years, many years, and we feared what the future might hold for us, wondering if it would ever be possible to laugh or be happy.

After each story everyone fell silent as they nodded, wiped tears, or clutched their hearts. The leader allowed just enough time for a long pause of understanding before signaling the next person to begin. Roger and I each told our story in our own words. Again, everyone nodded the now familiar nod of understanding. Every person in the room understood what we were experiencing. The fact our child was he before becoming she did not matter in the least. There were no questions, or so much as a raised brow, only sad solemn nods. Our child was dead, just like theirs. Nothing else mattered.

Heartsick and even more depressed, we left the meeting knowing full well we would return. The power of the group was obvious. It was oddly comforting to tell our story and put our grief, along with the grief of others, into a circle of support. The strangers we met the first night became a lifeline. They were the only people who understood, truly understood, the experience of losing a child.

Newcomers to the Circle of Gloom

There we were, gathered in the basement room.
Hovering about in a space between
Everyday life and harsh reality.
Zombies vaguely accustomed to being
Between what is and what was.
Reluctantly we welcomed each newcomer
Into our realm.
The heaviness of gloom and sadness
Circled our collective souls,
Spinning around us, impossible to escape.

There is no escape from the world of in-between.
Only brief visits to the edge,
Outside the circle of gloom.
No other circle fits so well now
As this circle of sadness
Where everyone knows
The unspoken language of grief
And offers a nod of understanding to the novice.

—KSL, December 1, 1999

Month after month that first year we returned to the comfort of this circle of gloom where no one said our child was in a better place, a stock phrase we often heard. They all knew the better place, the only place for their child, was here on earth, alive and well. Parents want to see their children grow, mature, and say good-bye to us when it is our time to leave. Jenni so wanted to be part of the future she dreamed about, not just a thing of the past. I wished time would heal, but I began to understand it would not. Anyone who loses a child knows life is forever changed, and grief never goes away. It just becomes somewhat more bearable.

Life indeed goes on, but even in times of celebrations, amidst feelings of tremendous gratitude and joy, there is a void that can never be filled except with memories. I doubt I will ever stop wishing Jenni were here with us, or wondering what she would be like in her thirties and forties, always wondering what if she were alive today. At those times, I take a deep breath, smile, tuck Jenni's memory inside me, and carry on with my life. That is all I can do.

Chapter 7

Acceptance

Acceptance is said to be the final stage of grief, the realization that life, newly defined, will go on. It does, and one can indeed laugh and be part of the world again. Time brings a new perspective and a deeper appreciation of life. The wound heals, but not without leaving a deep and painful scar. Roger re-framed the *time will heal* adage we heard so often to say it will never hurt less, but eventually it will hurt less often. So many years later as I write this, I could not agree more. Time can never heal so deep a wound as losing a child; time just makes it different. Our lives will never be the same, nor will they be as imagined. The reality of death - the death of a child- remains forever, even as we embrace the present and find joy in our existence.

In the first hours after the fateful phone call, I sped through the stages of grief. *Denial* is the first. Maybe, just maybe, if I don't acknowledge *it*, maybe *it* did not really happen. There was no kind police officer bringing the news to our door that awful night, staying until a family member or friend could be with us. There was just the phone call from three thousand miles away. Roger and I made our way downstairs to tell Sarah. Huddled together, we cried until there were no more tears, and the need to sleep became overpowering. Our bodies told us to prepare for what lay ahead and we had no choice but to listen.

I awoke first, went to the kitchen, swept the floor, and tidied up while I waited until daybreak before making calls to break the news. My family tradition was to announce a death as soon as it occurred. Uncles suddenly felled by heart attack or stroke, or grandparents finally succumbing to disease or old-age. I learned to brace myself to hear bad news whenever the phone rang, especially if it rang in the middle of the night. To this day I find it difficult to ignore a ringing phone. Answering always takes precedence over manners. Every call must be answered.

That morning, I resisted making the calls I knew I had to make. I wanted to believe if I did not tell anyone, the call would be part of a dream, a dreadful, horrible nightmare. Telling would only confirm the truth I was not ready to face. Yet somehow, in a state of shock, I began to make calls, bracing myself for reactions while still not in control of my own. I knew right then this day would mark the end of life as we knew it, the beginning of a life we never imagined. There was no denying it. I could not sweep it away with my broom, gather it into a dustbin, and go on as if the phone never rang that night.

I was too numb to be angry. *Anger* was futile. There was no one to blame and it would not change what happened. I was powerless to turn back the clock to tell Jenni not to get into her car when we spoke just before the accident. *Guilt* was not an option – there was nothing I could have done from three thousand miles away to prevent what happened. Long ago I learned life is not fair and terrible things happen, often without warning. My father's early death taught me that lesson.

Having sped through all the stages of grief in those early hours of daybreak, the final stage of *acceptance* was inevitable. Telling made it true. Jenni's death was sudden, swift, and unexpected. Death presented itself as a reality, a harsh terrible reality which had to be accepted. It was not negotiable. There was no going back, no option to return to the comfort of sleep, to dream another dream uninterrupted by a phone call. This was real. My child was dead. I made the calls. People arrived.

When Jenni came out to us, she was patient, and I was able to take time lingering through each stage of grief and analyze it as I mourned the loss of my son, the boy I raised, or so I thought. Jenni helped me understand what life was like for a person born in the wrong body. Acceptance brought joy in understanding transition was the right thing, the only thing for her. She was happy to finally live as the person she was meant to be, and I was confident our relationship now as mother and daughter would grow through the years. Her last hug at the airport, and our last conversation confirmed the strength of our bond. These two precious events played over and over in my head, reminding me of memories I would cherish forever.

It would have been unbearable had I not accepted her transition before being faced with the reality of her sudden death. I wanted to shout out to parents everywhere to love and accept their children. Being gay, or lesbian, or transgender is not terrible. It is neither a sin, nor a reason to reject, abuse, or shun your child. I wished everyone would open their minds to understand that there are many ways to be a human being, many ways to have a loving relationship, and many ways to construct a family. If only I could tell anyone who rejects a child for not living up to their expectations, to imagine something just for a moment. What if your children were to die and you still did not accept him or her?

We always have a choice to accept or reject change, just as it is a choice to embrace the possibilities life has to offer. Death gives us no choice - it must be accepted. Nonetheless, how one copes is a choice. Through my grief of first losing my son, and then the daughter she became, I gained a new perspective on life. For that I felt privileged.

During those months after Jenni's death, sitting on our porch in quiet contemplation gave me comfort. I remembered the sweet times we all sat there together as a family watching the rain, clutching each other as protection from thunder and lightning, or just waiting for night to fall and the stars to appear. Jenni and I sat on the porch the evening before she was to go back to California after her last visit home. With her head on my lap, we talked for hours. Suddenly an intense feeling of well-being washed over me as many of my maternal concerns dissipated, yet I knew they would never go away completely.

It was the *Ah-ha* moment when a parent breathes a sigh of relief knowing her child has been successfully launched into the adult world. Transitioning to another gender is grueling. It begins with learning to accept oneself and having the courage to change. I admired my child for her courage to change what she knew must be changed. Jenni was healthy and happy, a good person, ethical, kind, and loving. This was all that mattered. As a bonus, she was successful in her profession. I was confident she would carve out a beautiful life for herself and the family she would create. What more could a mother want for her child, except to be outlived by many more years.

After Jenni died, an unusual yellow bird, too large to be a common finch, made frequent appearances near our house. No one had ever seen one quite like it in our neighborhood. Several times the little visitor soared past me and circled back as if to tell me Jenni was everywhere, in the wind and in the trees. She was a colorful butterfly reveling in its freedom to fly rather than crawl. She was a yellow bird soaring through the sky. I took comfort wherever I could find it.

Chapter 8

Letting Go

Always industrious, Sarah earned enough money with after school jobs to purchase a 1974 Volkswagen Beetle, her dream car. It was in sorry condition, but with the help of her auto shop teacher and classmates, she lovingly restored it using skills she learned in class and on her own. The summer of Jenni's death, she had plans to drive across country with her third cousin, Anna, to visit Jenni in California. Anna's great-grandfather, Ruben, and Sarah's paternal great-grandfather, Louis, whom I knew as *Zaide*, were brothers. Unable to gain entry to the United States, Ruben settled in England where he too raised a large family.

The girls' departure date had been scheduled for the week after Sarah finished her classes in Manhattan, less than a month after Jenni's death. Anna arrived from London, and the girls were determined to leave as planned. Given the circumstances and fearing for the safety of two young women travelling alone, I desperately wanted them to cancel the trip, yet I could not insist they stay. I tried, but all of my protests were countered with logical rebuttals.

The car was in good running order, Sarah was an excellent driver, and she was certainly competent enough to handle most emergency situations and repairs. Nonetheless, I was terrified. Another loss would be unbearable. Unrealistic as it was, I wanted my family physically close to me. I felt helpless, far away from Jenni when she died, powerless to stop Sarah from going ahead with her plans. Yet, I understood her need to run from her traumatized parents while she grappled with the loss of her sister, who was once her older brother.

The day my father died, my first impulse was to run as fast as my legs would carry me. In and out of a canopy of trees in a neighborhood park, I ran until I could run no further. My cousin David, two years my senior, was sent to follow me and escort me home. When he caught up, we walked together in silence. No words were necessary. I understood on a very deep, non-verbal level that he knew exactly how I felt - confused, frightened, alone. His father, my father's brother, suffered a fatal stroke just three years before my father collapsed on our living room floor. Now I knew what he knew, and I was grateful for his presence. My tears, as well as the shame I felt about a silly adolescent argument I had with my father the day before, had stayed buried for years.

Intellectually I knew my father's death was unrelated, but the guilt on top of the trauma of loss overshadowed my memories of an otherwise happy childhood with two loving parents, an older sister, aunts, uncles, and cousins. Yet the good memories, of which there had been many, remain hardest to retrieve. The calls in the middle of the night, the mourning periods, the feeling of being a deer caught in the headlights, stunned and helpless, overshadowed them for decades. Now as I reflect on my family tree I recognize a strong tendency to cope and make the best of life, seeking joy at every opportunity, knowing full well it can end at any moment.

The summer of my junior year of college, I set off on an adventure to declare my independence and escape the sadness of my widowed mother. With a copy of Frommer's *Europe on Five Dollars a Day* and a two-month rail pass for unlimited travel, I left my mother, each of us alone for the first time in our lives. Given the perspective of time, I can only imagine her anguish while I was travelling. She was a worrier. I try not to be, but I resigned myself to the fact that it is passed on from generation to generation. Despite her fears, my mother bravely let me go off on a foreign adventure while she patiently waited for the blue aerograms I sent a few times a week to describe my adventures with assurance I was okay, albeit a week or more after the fact.

Harnessing my mother's spirit, I let Sarah go, confident that her traveling companion would be there at her side to listen when she needed to talk, and just be there for her. I helped the two girls pack the car with food and emergency supplies. I might even have made cookies. Roger's cousin who came to visit and see Sarah off, reminded me of the stack of cucumber and cream cheese sandwiches on raisin bread we had prepared at their request.

My daughter needed to go, and I needed to let her go, just as my mother had let me go. I forced myself to understand it was a journey she needed to take to distance herself from my grief, just as I had once needed to distance myself from my mother's sadness. While they were gone, I waited for the call I insisted upon receiving every day to be assured they arrived safely at each destination. Anna was usually the one to make the call. I forced myself to understand my daughter's reluctance to talk as a protective cloak of numbness which might be compromised by conversations with her parents. I wanted to be there for Sarah with a shoulder to rest her head and a tissue to dry her tears, the things my mother could not do for me.

So consumed by her own grief, my mother had been unable to comfort me when my father died. A mother myself now, I wondered if my child held back her tears, as I held back mine when my father died. My own tears for my father took nearly two years to burst through after his death. It took nearly forty years to write of that loss as I filled the pages of my journals in the months and years after Jenni's death.

Days of Bread and Babka

Every Friday of my childhood the aroma of freshly baked breads and cakes permeated the stairwells and hallways of our apartment building in New Jersey, just across the river from Manhattan. It was a marble stair-cased, red-brick, pre-war structure surrounded by private homes, just a few blocks from a large county park. After school, I could barely wait to put down my books and hurry into the kitchen of our spacious apartment. The kitchen table would be covered with my mother's creations – a braided challah, a babka filled with cinnamon, raisins, and walnuts, and sometimes simple cake. I always hoped for frosting to lick from the beaters, but that was only an occasional treat.

My mother loved to bake. As she measured and stirred, she would marvel at the delicate balance of ingredients and the chemistry of the mixtures. The yellow Sunbeam electric mixer, one of the first of its kind, was busy every Friday. After doing its job it was cleaned, covered with a plastic bonnet, and stowed away on a shelf above the stove. As I look at the same mixer, forty years later, displayed atop my kitchen cabinets, I remember those days of bread and babka.

They were forgotten for a long time. Those dormant memories are likely responsible for my own fascination with baking, but somehow, even with the same recipes, mine never smell or taste the same. By the time I was interested in learning to bake, years past those days when I was given bits of dough to roll and form into little cakes as I sat in a high chair, my mother had lost interest in doing what she so enjoyed. The babka was but a memory. The challah, a relic from a past long gone when my mother lit Sabbath candles before the Friday night meal as our little family gathered -- my mother, father, older sister, and sometimes a cousin, who worked at the newspaper with my father.

The sudden death of my father brought an end to the Friday rituals. That day remains etched in my memory as other memories faded. It was the first day of summer vacation from school. He awoke feeling ill. Suddenly short of breath, he collapsed on the floor. Cradling him in our arms, my mother, my sister and I talked to him as we waited for the ambulance which arrived in slow motion, too late to save him. It was an abrupt end of a life, and the end of life as we knew it. A large black trunk, already packed for my upcoming first summer camp experience, was unpacked. Camp was out of the question, as we embarked on a summer of mourning.

My mother, who had enjoyed the luxury of not working outside of her home, was thrust into economic need. Abruptly she stopped doing what she loved and what my father encouraged her to do. She was no longer interested in those magical mixes of simple ingredients and she gave up singing in the synagogue choir. The melodies and the sounds of the ancient lyrics had intrigued her, even though she did not know their meaning. She stopped painting in the local art league studio in the penthouse of our apartment building. Her still life in oils had won first prize in a county show. My father had arranged press coverage of the event. Suddenly and abruptly, all her creativity was sacrificed for the practicalities of becoming the sole provider for her family.

My sister's wedding, scheduled for the next year, went ahead as planned. For the first time in my life, I had my own room, but that too came to an abrupt end. Six months later, my mother and I moved to Queens, to a place in New York where the skyline of Manhattan was no longer visible. A more affordable apartment in a post-war housing development near my aunt, my mother's sister, became available. It was small, with only one bedroom. In the middle of my junior year of high school we packed up, leaving friends and family behind. I learned everything in life is transient, like the aroma of freshly baked bread.

The memories of those familiar, but long-gone scents of childhood were triggered years after my father's death in a place he had never been. It was a Friday afternoon. Opening the front door to the apartment building, I was greeted by the same familiar aroma I remembered from my childhood. It filled every pore of my body, touching my soul, pushing me past the elevator to the stairwell. I nearly flew up the three flights of stairs, tears streaming from my eyes. Would I find cakes or bread - anything, anything would do. I opened the door. The apartment was empty. Someone else in the building was baking. Sobbing uncontrollably, I dropped to the floor and stayed there until it was time to prepare dinner for my mother who would soon be home from work.

—KSL, March 1999

The death of my father taught me how to deal with loss. Brace yourself against the pain. Put away the grief. Don't let it out. Go on with life. We did the best we could. But losing a child is different and

I wanted to be comforted. To this day, many years after my mother's death, I sometimes start for the phone to call her when there is good news to share, or to let her know I returned safely home from a trip, or sometimes, just to hear her voice. I try to imagine her response when I wonder if time will ever heal the pain of losing a child. I now know her answer. Go on with life, just as she did, savor memories, try to be positive and appreciative. And keep my child's spirit alive always.

* * * * *

Jenni's accident as it was described to us replayed over and over in my mind. The sight of a white sports car on a highway conjured up images, in slow motion, of Jenni's car drifting across three lanes of traffic, hitting the divider, bouncing in the air, turning over, and dropping upside down on the pavement. Traffic stood still for hours. Without seeing the photographs that documented the accident, the scene remains vivid, even to this day.

Not long after Jenni's death, a television commercial featuring a white Miata racing around a curve until it was swallowed up by a giant wave out of nowhere, aired frequently. A little boy formally dressed in a suit, appeared in front of the wave to declare in a flat voice, devoid of emotion, *Zoom. Zoom. Zoom.* It was torture to watch. Jenni disappeared in a wave, in a flash, gone forever. This was not child's play. It was not a Zoom, Zoom moment.

When Sarah returned from her trip, neither of us could talk about it. It - the trip. It - the grief. It - the accident. It - the terrible, terrible loss. Instead, we spent precious time together, times I will cherish. Her summer school professors offered to allow her to drop out with no mark left on her record dues to the circumstances, but she was determined to finish her classes and complete her final projects. For one class, her research took her to community gardens which had been popping up in alleyways and empty lots throughout Manhattan. I was thrilled that she asked me to join her. We walked, often in silence, from one garden to another and sat next each other as she jotted down her observations. It was time I cherished.

One evening Sarah asked if I would teach her how to follow a pattern for making comfortable pants to take back to school. I wrote about it few months later, along with a flood of childhood memories which swept over me.

* * * * *

In Kindergarten, I drew a picture of clothes hanging on a clothesline - a pair of pants, a dress, socks, and a sheet. Each one carefully colored within the boundaries I drew. My mother loved that drawing– it hung in our kitchen for a very, very long time. She thought it was brilliant. I moved on.

My parents came of age during the Great Depression. Thrift was part of their nature, and money was spent carefully. Except for the occasional treat of a special toy, I entertained myself for hours with stacks of newsprint from the newspaper where my father worked. Scissors, crayons, and a piece of cardboard that came from the laundry where my father's shirts were occasionally sent to be washed, ironed, and starched were all I really needed. The coveted pieces of cardboard were reserved for making a cut-out of a person to be dressed in paper dresses attached by tabs at the top and sides. Commercial books of cut-out dolls that sometimes came my way as gifts were an inspiration, not ends unto themselves.

Money was tight during my college years and I was glad the 1960's styles were easy to make – no zippers, no buttons, only drawstrings. A far too short, orange halter dress with yellow flowers caught Roger's eye on campus. My handmade dress and the paper flower he bought from me months before at the pharmacy where I worked on weekends brought us together. I recognized the flower I had made at his apartment when I stopped there with a friend who was looking for his roommate.

We encouraged our children to be creative. Don't buy it – you can make it. Sometimes, it was out of necessity. We didn't buy software for Joshua's first computer, a Commodore 64 for his tenth birthday - it was far too expensive at the time. Thus he learned to program and he invented his own games. First, a typing tutor, then a space game, and later a program for tracking stock market high and low cycles. We let him invest some money he had saved. Every morning before school, he checked his investments, buying or selling, based on the program's predictions. We cheered as his portfolio grew.

Sarah learned to embellish her clothing and piece together simple garments. Always meticulous, she mastered everything she set out to learn – knitting, crocheting, quilting, repairing and restoring cars. When she was twelve years old, we bought her bedroom furniture which required assembly. On the pretext of going to sleep early, she kissed us good-night, and went upstairs to her room. There she opened each box of furniture parts, read the directions, and got to work assembling almost all the pieces by herself, working well into the night. In the morning, we found her asleep on the floor.

At the end of this terrible summer of grief, Sarah asked me to teach her how to use a pattern to make clothing. We shopped for fabric and assembled paper pattern pieces on the dining room table. I taught her what I learned in a class in clothing construction, an elective I took in college. Follow each direction in order, and never skip a step. Every seam must be pressed open and flat. Finish each and every edge.

Sarah and I cut and sewed all evening, silent as we worked. We were exhausted, but pleased with the three pairs of pants we made and the new skill acquired. As I started upstairs to head for bed, I heard a familiar little girl voice coming from my now grown-up daughter.

"Mommy, let's sit on the porch for a while before we go to bed."

We talked. We wept. We held each other tight. If only I could mend her broken heart. We both knew I could not, any more than she could mend mine. Eventually, a sense of calm enveloped us as we sat in silence. There we were, late at night, two women, mother and daughter, comforting each other as we struggled to make sense of life and death.

—KSL, December 1998

* * * * *

My grandmother had a habit of repackaging dry food into jars. The cooking instructions on boxes of rice, kasha, farina, and tiny bowtie noodles were carefully cut out and attached by rubber bands to each jar. My mother loved her visits, but hated her mother's habit of rearranging the pantry. She had no trouble expressing her exasperation as soon as Grandma left. I was a young child when I first observed my mother, a grown woman, rebelling against her mother.

When Roger and I returned from a year living on a kibbutz in Israel, penniless, unemployed, and pregnant, my mother did everything she could to help out. Somehow an extra chicken or an extra bunch of broccoli would end up in her shopping cart. She said she didn't know how it happened – what was she to do with it? I didn't want to take it and let her know, even at the expense of hurting her feelings. After all I was a grown woman and wanted to do everything my way.

My grandmother and mother are long gone, and I am the mother of a grown woman. I buy nuts and grains in bulk at the grocery and store them in my pantry in glass jars, mostly recycled, with instructions rubber banded in place. I sometimes bring food I've prepared to my busy daughter and tell her with a smile that I don't know how it happened, but I wound up making too much, or somehow, something extra fell in the cart. She knows the story.

These moments of shared intergenerational connection are precious, very precious, but yet, after all these years, nearly twenty now, I imagine Jenni's smile if I were to appear on her doorstep with a jar of soup. Such thoughts vanish as quickly as they appear. Instead I try to focus on the present moment, the moments I have now, and the memories I make today, now all the more precious.

Karen Shiffman Lateiner

Chapter 9

Dance of Life

The day of the accident Jenni had intended to drop off film to be developed. Jenni and Margaret spent a day at the beach the weekend prior to the accident, taking photos of one another. Margaret had one of the photos enlarged for us. It is a remarkable image of Jenni leaping through the air, leaving a shadow reflected in the water. I look at it every day, feeling sad, feeling peaceful, and feeling glad that Jenni experienced such happiness, reveling in her intense love of life with the love of her life.

She Danced on the Beach

She danced on the beach.
A dance of joy...twirling, twirling,
Encompassing the sun, the clouds, the wind,
And all the wonders of the world in each grain of sand.
She inhaled life, delighted in all it could offer,
In all she could give.
She danced and danced to the music of the universe.
The wind. The waves.
With life, with love, and with every soul
Whose life she touched.

Now the beach is empty.
The sun, the clouds, the sand remains forever.
She will never dance upon the beach again.
Perhaps she'll dance through eternity,
Invisible, but everywhere.
Wherever we feel her presence.
Her dance of life continues within us
In the music of the waves.

Her soul released on the beach,
Released forever on the highway,
Released in the funeral pyre.
Released to the universe.

—KSL, October 19, 1998

Margaret took us to the same beach near Santa Cruz when we returned to California to sort through Jenni's belongings. With reverence and in silence we approached the water. I found a place to sit in a small cave in the rocks while Roger walked along the beach, each of us alone in our thoughts. Out of nowhere it seemed, a handsome, mocha-skinned man in flowing pants and loose shirt appeared in the place I imagined Jenni had danced her dance of joy. He dropped his shirt in the sand and began to dance on the beach, seemingly oblivious of my presence in the shadow. He danced a dance of life, of love, of oneness with the universe. The dance was feminine and flowing, moving like the wind, rhythmic as the waves. This beautiful stranger finished his dance and walked away without a word, a nod, or even a smile. I wondered who he was and where he came from, but knew it did not matter. His message was clear. The dance continues. I sensed this graceful stranger, the dancer from nowhere, came to release his soul to the universe as Jenni released hers in her dance.

Stunned by the enormity of the past months, there was little we could say on the plane ride home. Roger stared out the window. He said he could almost imagine Jenni swooping through the clouds, giggling and having fun. We laughed at the thought, wishing it were so, seeking any notion that would give us comfort, even the most far-fetched.

Back home, writing groups provided solace as we meditated and wrote what came to mind. When it was time to share our words, we listened and reflected. Sometimes there was something to say. Sometimes there was nothing anyone could say. Often we sat in silence, sharing the pain, or joy, or sorrow in our short narratives. Someone in the group told us about a little girl who wrote about her beloved deceased cat to make her live again. This child knew the ways of the universe. We are the keepers of spirits. By telling their stories, we keep our loved ones alive. This was a lesson my mother taught me with stories of her own first child who lived for only two days, or her inventive, funny, brilliant brother who died when was just sixteen, or her uncles who played mandolins and told jokes, all of their spirits adding richness to our family history.

I dreaded the approach of November 9, 1998, Jenni's twenty-fifth birthday, the first of many birthdays we would miss. Roger and I drove to Ohio to be together with Sarah. It was the only way for us to get through this day we knew would be especially difficult. We could not let Jenni's birthday pass without celebrating it as a memorial to her. We decided to bring along a box of chocolate truffles, rather than a cake, which would have seemed out of place for a celebration without the guest of honor. The last time we spent time together as a family, Jenni ran into a shop to buy fancy chocolates to eat as we strolled through the streets of Sausalito. On this sad day, Roger, Sarah and I sat together in a restaurant in the little town of Oberlin, with room at the table for Jenni's spirit. We ate breakfast of eggs, toast, and chocolate truffles, conjuring up memories, forcing ourselves to laugh, wishing Jenni were with us, not believing we would never see her again.

Roger and I drove home in a daze. It always seemed to rain on the way home from Ohio, through Pennsylvania to New Jersey on Route 80, where trucks far outnumbered cars. We dared not share our thoughts on that long drive home. My thoughts that stormy night we celebrated Jenni's birthday without her spilled out later in the week.

The Scream

I'm numb. I feel nothing. I'm so afraid of releasing again that awful scream, the scream that forced my body into a grotesque pose on that terrible night, the night the phone rang. My body convulsed. I had to move. Or I would be left in that pose forever, as if a statue, never knowing how my body could so bend and twist. My legs would not hold me. That scream again would turn me inside out — leaving only a shell, an exposed shell of a human being whose life in a moment was forever altered, robbed of the future as planned, as dreamed, as hoped.

I'm numb. The scream wants to come out again but cannot. It would take everything out of me. I'm numb. I contain the scream with a body committed to living, to continuance, erecting memorials in stone, in living trees, in daffodils for all the neighbors to plant in memory of my child. Spring will come and the daffodils will grow, full of life, full of sadness. She will never see their cheerful smiles, and I will never see hers. I cook and bake, just like my mother did, as my past comes back in a flood of memories. I write them on scraps of paper. All the past pains and losses. All the past screams I buried within.

I'm numb. I seek life where there is emptiness, something to fill the void, the terrible, terrible loss. I remember my father snatched from life, suddenly, as his family embraced him. That moment of his death erased all memory of him. Yet the moment of his death remains etched in my mind. Now memories begin to return. He was a quiet man. A pharmacist turned journalist, with a passion for news. I remember when I was very young visiting the newspaper where he worked, my little hand clutching his. He proudly showed me off, introduced me to all the other newspapermen. I watched in awe as giant machines belched out the day's news. The noise of teletype and typesetting machines was overwhelming to a child's ear. The men at the linotype machines set the letters of my name in metal - in small, medium, and large type. A cherished souvenir displayed on my bookshelf, their obsolete meaning lost to most.

On weekends, my father wrote a column for the local newspaper. Two fingers flying so fast they were barely visible. Sweat dripping from his brow. He worked with an intensity mapped on his genes passed on to the grandchildren he never met. When he died so young, so swift, my scream was squelched. I held it inside. I became numb. I forgot all the treasured moments, buried under that scream. With each release, more memories escape, some retrieved, some flee forever.

I'm numb. I am numb with memories long hidden finally released in words. Is this my father's legacy? My path set in genetic material unyielding to alternative direction.

—*KSL, November 11, 1998*

Memories continued to flood my mind. I wrote about everything but Jenni. It was too new, too painful, and I was too raw. The wounds of my past needed to be reconciled before acknowledging the gaping hole in my heart. Five years before Jenni's death my mother died, and only one month prior to her death, Roger's father died. His mother died five years before. Fifty years old and I was still not ready to take on the mantle of being an elder with a perspective on life based on experience.

The days, months, and even those first years continued as a blur. I constructed an invisible, impenetrable bubble to protect myself from falling apart. Going through the motions of daily life, I imagined time passing differently for those outside my reality. People peered inside, but few were able to connect. I consoled those whose eyes welled up when they saw me, or when I told my story, hugging and comforting them rather than letting them break through my protective bubble.

I was fortunate to have close friends who nurtured me with kindness and listened when I wanted to talk, freely offering warm embraces and a shoulder on which to cry. Yet, there were those who carefully avoided me in shops and on the street. My mother reported that she experienced the same curious phenomenon after my father died. It took years for me to understand it not so much as shunning, but as a reminder of the fragility of life, a reality far too painful to contemplate. For some, it might be easier, or even necessary, to walk away rather than confront someone who is grieving, reminding them that person could be anyone, could be them.

Some of our cousins hesitated to tell their elderly parents of Jenni's transition, thinking they would have a difficult time understanding what they themselves struggled to comprehend. Quite the opposite proved to be the case. A few weeks after Jenni's death, Roger and I visited my Aunt Molly, my father's younger half-sister. She was too frail to travel, but wanted to see us. Supporting herself with a walker, her neck in a brace, she led us outside to sit in the garden of the nursing home where she lived. We talked and showed her photographs of Jenni. She studied each one. After a while she took my hand and looking deeply in my eyes, and said, *You must wish you had your mother here now – I'm glad I can be here for you.*

There were no tears, just the three of us silently holding each other's hands as we absorbed the wisdom of time. We learned later that she instructed her own adult children to understand what they had thought she could never comprehend, reminding them keep in contact with us, stay close, and remember that Joshua was always Jennifer, Jenni, and should be remembered as such. They did, and we continue to cherish my wise aunt's words and the warmth of her children.

Far too soon after Jenni's death, we attended a celebration for my older cousin whose positive outlook on life remains inspiration. Even now in his nineties, my cousin Harvey reminds us to *do as much as you can for as long as you can.* That day we were welcomed with love and support, but still I could not shake the feeling our presence was a black cloud that stopped conversation as people searched for things to say. Some months later, Roger and I mustered up the courage to attend a family wedding. We tried to pretend life had returned to normal and joined our family to celebrate this joyous event. The band played *Sunrise, Sunset* with its heartfelt refrain – *Is This the Little Girl I Carried? Is This The Little Boy at Play?*

The words struck us like daggers. As everyone stood up to dance, we slipped outside, far enough away so as not to be heard, to hold each other and release a torrent of tears. It was too soon. *It takes time*, the phrase we heard so often, not necessarily to heal, but to make it possible to participate fully in life, although life would never be the same.

Chapter 10

Life Goes On

Not long before the accident, I abandoned my doctoral studies in educational psychology. When Jenni came out, my need to learn everything I could about what it means to be transgender overshadowed my research in infant development. I no longer had the energy to jump through academic hoops, which at the time seemed to move at random the closer I got to the end. My personal journey as a mother whose son became her daughter expanded my mind and sparked my interest far beyond the confines of graduate school and my research, all of which no longer seemed relevant. Before seeking employment beyond the halls of academia, I took time to process the enormity of events which impacted my life.

Around the turn of the twentieth century, all of my grandparents had the foresight to leave Europe for America, the land of opportunity, leaving behind the hardships facing them as Jews. Many of my relatives who stayed in Europe likely perished during pogroms or later during the Holocaust. No one except my mother talked about the family left behind and what might have happened to them. So many people of my parent's generation, first generation as well as survivors kept silent for decades. Memories of hate, destruction, and genocide were too painful. Many thought it best to keep silent, remembering their loved ones in prayer and contemplation. Silence protected them as they learned to appreciate life, gain perspective, and develop a sense of humor. Somehow people survive, stumbling along, muddling through, finding joy and trying to make sense of it all. Life is full of loss. There is no escape.

I learned to appreciate more than ever before, long walks with friends in our neighborhood park, a place where century-old trees bore witness to countless stories, keeping as many secrets. One day, in all innocence a friend commented on generations past when women had many children, knowing few would survive. She conjectured their grief might have been less profound than mine. After all, they expected death and were used to it.

What? I thought. *Does anyone ever get used to the death of a child, or do they just manage to go on living?* Throughout history, infants and children died, sometimes one after another. It is impossible to imagine any mother's grief for a child, no matter the age at death, or how many children were left behind, could be any less than mine. Somehow we survive and go on with our lives, but I doubt we ever stop wondering what might have been. Silently, we accept our fate making the choice to carry on, grateful for what is, never forgetting what was.

* * * * *

A few years after my father's death, my mother exclaimed in a voice not meant for me to hear as she sobbed into her hands, *What's the use of living?* She was grieving and understandably sad. Confused and vulnerable from the trauma of witnessing my father's death, moving to a new city, and leaving friends, her words frightened me. I was afraid for her. Despite knowing she was determined to build a life, provide for herself, and send me off to college, I hesitated to leave her alone and chose to remain at home to attend a local college.

We shared a bedroom and a closet in our tiny apartment. My embroidered blouses, jeans, and mini-skirts hung on one side, her housedresses and polyester pantsuits on the other. She found enjoyment in her work and in the stories I chose to share with her. We went on with life, as cheerfully as we could as our grief lingered in the background. I'll never know how my life might have unfolded had I not heard her words of despair. I had planned to go away to college and live abroad for a semester or two. Had I done that, my mother might have developed her own social circle; maybe she would have dated, or remarried. She was still young, only fifty when my father died.

One evening, while washing dishes in our tiny apartment, a plate slipped from my hand and shattered into the sink. For the first time, I expressed my frustration, not about breaking the plate, but about what happened to our lives. Without a word, my mother rose from her chair in the next room, opened the cupboard door, and handed me a stack of old plates to be thrown into the sink. She watched as I threw one after another before joining me to throw in more plates, each one shattering just as our lives had shattered. After surveying the damage, we held each other and sobbed, not for the dishes, but for ourselves. And then we laughed. With a long, deep breath and firm resolve, we cleaned up the mess and went on with our lives.

Karen Shiffman Lateiner

Chapter 11

Reality Sets In

As soon as they arrived, I gathered the strength to read the police and autopsy reports from Jenni's accident. She was traveling at the speed limit along with traffic on the highway where the accident occurred. Witnesses reported seeing the car in front of them, Jenni's car, veer across three lanes of traffic, hit the divider, fly through the air, skid along the highway, and land upside down on the road. No other cars were involved. The autopsy was negative for drugs or alcohol, and there was no evidence of a cerebral or cardiac event which could have interfered with Jenni's ability to drive, however we wondered if evidence of a cerebral event might have been masked by the physical damage from the accident. No one could tell us, but ultimately it did not matter. Nothing could change what happened. Yet, I still had questions.

The driver fell asleep was stated as the official cause of the accident. It seemed incongruous. Jenni had apparently left her house a half hour or so after we spoke, and hours before we were notified. Ironically, when Jenni first moved to California she told us about the reflector bumps separating lanes on highways. She thought it was a brilliant idea to warn drivers if their attention lapsed and they drifted into another lane, the sudden unevenness of the road sure to bring a driver back to focus. I could not help but wonder why those very bumps failed to alert Jenni in time.

I called the police officer who wrote the report. I remembered him as kind and compassionate when he met us in California at the place where Jenni's car was impounded for investigation. He had been there to officially release Jenni's belongings and learn more about her. I asked if it were possible that Jenni had reached over to change the station on the radio, or to find something in her purse. He said it was unlikely. Rather, he explained that the evidence showed no sign of a correction in an attempt to avoid hitting the divider, as would be expected in such a situation. The negative autopsy, the lack of mechanical problems or skid marks on the road, and the eyewitness reports that Jenni's head seemed to bob just prior to the accident, added together confirmed their conclusion that she fell asleep.

As part of his investigation, the police officer talked to Jenni's friends and co-workers. He told us friends and colleagues described Jenni as exceptionally brilliant. There was genuine sadness in his voice as he expressed sincere sorrow for our loss. I wished he had been the one to break the news that our child was dead rather than the medical examiner, not that it would have been any easier, but it would have been more compassionate.

Another day, I called Jenni's doctor in San Francisco, to tell her what happened. I wondered if the medications and the hormones she was taking to transform her body from male to female might have caused a blackout. The doctor did not think so. She went on to say that in her years of working in emergency room settings, before devoting her practice to transgender patients, she had seen hundreds of teenagers and young adults who had experienced a seizure, an abnormal electrical event in the brain. For many, it was a unique and solitary event resulting in a momentary blackout that might have lasted seconds, or a few minutes. In a safe setting, the consequences might be minimal, but behind the wheel of a car, potentially disastrous. She went on to say that in most cases, the cause of these momentary blackouts remained a mystery, often leaving no trace to be discovered on autopsy. This seemed a more plausible explanation, even if could not be confirmed. I needed a reason why my child had a lapse of attention that caused her death.

Somehow, I mustered up the strength to call the coroner's office to speak to the pathologist who performed the autopsy. I had more questions about the report, but mostly I was compelled to ask if it was standard procedure for the medical examiner to call the family about a loved one's death, rather than notify a local police department to break the news. I wanted to share my impression of the caller as cold and callous, almost annoyed, definitely ill-suited to deliver dreadful news. He listened.

In a soft kind voice, he said he was truly sorry for our loss. What else could he say to a grieving parent? I hoped my feedback would lead to conversations about the impact of language and tone in announcing the death of a loved one, especially from so far away. It is difficult, but I believe not impossible to teach compassion and empathy, or at least talk about it. I wondered if bias or prejudice towards a transgender person played a role. If so, there is all the more reason to begin what can be controversial and difficult conversations.

When I think about how I made those calls, I recall the surreal scene of my mother standing in the kitchen offering to make coffee for the doctor, a family friend, who had just pronounced my father, lifeless on the floor in the next room, dead. My mother apologized for waking him in the middle of the night before asking a series of questions about what could have caused her husband, my father, to die so suddenly. She was direct and detached - no doubt in shock. Years later, after the death of my child, I, like my mother, was able to detach to ask questions and do what I needed to do.

One night, in the room which still echoed from the call in the middle of the night, I read and re-read the police report. Two women, independent of each other, had stopped their cars to run to the little sports car upside down on the highway in front of them. Through tears, I gathered the strength to call these strangers. Each reported that they talked to Jenni, trying in vain to comfort her with words as they touched her arm and felt the last faint pulsing of her veins. The officer who responded to the accident, the one I spoke to after reading the autopsy report, reported it was too late by the time he arrived. One woman was unsure if the driver was male or female, but knew it did not matter. She was certain she saw a white light rise from the car. It left her with an overwhelming sense that a powerful spirit had left the earth. I told her about Jenni, confirming her impression. We sobbed together on the phone.

Ten years before Jenni died, I had what might have been almost a near-death experience at the end of a family trek from the bottom of the Grand Canyon where we spent two glorious days exploring Havasupai Falls. It was summer in the desert - dry and hot. I was dehydrated and probably hypoglycemic as I struggled to make my way up the last leg of the steep switchback trails to the parking lot at the trailhead. An intense desire to become part of the earth overwhelmed me. I wanted to lie down and rest, sink into the rocks, and surrender completely to the sense of well-being I felt wash over me. Roger and Sarah brought me back to reality pushing me to complete the last leg of the journey while Joshua shouted encouraging words from the top.

I left the Canyon that day with a powerful impression of the peacefulness reported to precede impending death. We survived that adventure, ready for the next – renting giant tire tubes to float down a river near Zion National Park in Utah. Joshua and I marveled at the view as we drifted ahead of Roger and Sarah. Looking up at the sky outlined by trees against the backdrop of massive red and golden cliffs, Joshua exclaimed - *This is heaven!* I can only hope that Jenni experienced a sense of peacefulness as her short life ended.

Karen Shiffman Lateiner

Chapter 12

A Powerful Spirit

I want to believe Jenni's last moments on earth were painless and serene. I no longer remember the names of those witnesses, but I can never forget their presence as my child drew her last breath, comforting her with human touch. I wonder if they remember. How could they forget?

Angels

What are these beings we call angels?
Do they swoop down from a world beyond?
Or dwell within us, always at the ready
To be there, unsummoned, but welcome.
They give nothing, but their presence
There to comfort, freely and unselfishly,
With no thought for themselves.

Two angels appeared when my child took her last breath,
Cradling her as she crossed the divide from life to death.
Leaving behind a dreadfully damaged body.
Her powerful spirit, her life force, joined the universe.
Such selflessness a gift transforming unspeakable images
Into reflections of serenity, and pure,
Unconditional human love.
The touch of these angels never forgotten.

—KSL, December 16, 1998

I never met either of these brave women. The box containing their names and phone numbers on the police report, as well as Jenni's address book, condolence cards, and memories remains untouched near my desk at home. Every so often, I lift the cover, peek inside and close the box again, still not ready to go back there, touch everything, and decide what to do with it all. Meanwhile, stacks of cartons remain in storage, the contents and accomplishments of a short life, stowed away to be sorted through and discarded...someday.

In the daily chores of life, I encountered acquaintances who had heard the sad news of Jenni's death. Sometimes they shared a memory or two. Some referred to her as Jenni, understanding she was always Jenni. Others could only refer to her as Joshua. No matter how they chose to remember my child, I treasure their memories as a confirmation she would not be forgotten.

A friend who knew Joshua from the time he was a little boy believed, as her faith taught her, that our child was in a better place. She shared a dream she had of Jenni, even though she had only known Joshua. In her dream, she saw Jenni as a child in a pink dress playing with a group of other little girls on a fluffy bed of clouds. A year later, at an art exhibit, a kitschy picture caught my eye. Just like the image in my friend's dream, it depicted a cherub in a pink tutu reaching for the sky from a bed of fluffy clouds. It would be nice to think Jenni is happily playing in the clouds. I do not believe it to be real, but the image makes me smile.

The mystery of how the accident happened, and why Jenni died, hardly matters. The fact is she is dead. Nothing can bring her back. Nothing can make her live again, but her spirit can live on forever in the hearts and minds of those who knew her, or knew of her. An artist friend told me I have an important job for the remainder of my life. She said it is my responsibility to keep Jenni's spirit alive and with me always, since without this notion of a spirit, there can be no artistic expression. My mother, also an artist, understood this concept.

It made perfect sense to me. We, the living, are entrusted to keep alive the spirits of loved ones to give them eternal life in the universe of memories. To some people, memories are so painful they are unable to talk about loved ones who have died. I had to talk about Jenni to keep her spirit alive, and tell her story to help change the way we think about gender and acceptance.

Jenni's spirit never ceases to be part of me, always present, always in the back of my mind, or fully in my consciousness. The eye-witness report of Jenni's spirit rising from the car as a white light gives me great comfort. I have to believe she felt the touch of another human being and experienced a sense of calm in those last moments. Anything else is torture. To this day I seek solace in the majestic landscape of the Southwest where we now live, with its endless mountains that appear to change colors with the light. Everyone's spirit seems to be here, safe in the colorful mountains that hold remains of ancient civilizations. I try to imagine Jenni's spirit drifting through the canyons of time to live on in memory, if only in the memory of the universe.

Karen Shiffman Lateiner

Chapter 13

Growing Up Joshua

Not a day goes by when I do not think about Jenni, or Joshua, depending upon the time frame remembered. At night, when I close my eyes to sleep, I see my child's infant face, neither male nor female, merely beautiful and innocent. Strangers stopping to coo at my baby often remarked he was too pretty to be a boy. Eyes like that should be on a girl they said.

Joshua grew to be an inquisitive, serious child, who seemed to have an understanding of the world well beyond his years. His eyes, dark as coal, appeared to hold memories yet to be verbalized. When he was nearly four years old, he pressed his ear against my belly to listen to his sibling growing inside. *There's a swimming pool in there. I went swimming there one day!* He exclaimed. I asked him what it was like when he came out. With a far off look and a shiver that vibrated through his little body he replied - *It was chilly.*

I asked what else there was. Silent and pensive, he looked up as if to a picture in his mind. Suddenly, almost triumphantly, as if he searched for and actually caught a memory, he said, *The room was blue. There were lots of people there.* Indeed, there were a lot of people there, and the room could very well have been a shade of hospital blue.

I wondered if Joshua actually remembered his birth and was finally able to put words to the pictures stored in his memory. Seeking answers, I went on to study infant development, but was unable to find any research to support my hypothesis that infants can remember their birth, and tell about it later. Nonetheless, the burgeoning research in infant development in the 1980s was fascinating to me, especially with regard to how children develop a sense of themselves and what is expected of them through interactions with their environment and how they are labeled at birth.

When Joshua was just about four years old, his beloved Barney, an over-sized teddy bear, began emitting unpleasant odors and we discussed what we might do. Together we decided to take Barney to the extra-large washing machines in the basement of our apartment building. As the giant bear tumbled in the washer and then circled around in the dryer, Joshua paced back and forth, hands together, saying over and over, *Please God, please, let Barney be okay.* Apparently he had learned to ask for divine intervention from one of his little friends, who showed him how to clasp his hands together and pray. Happily, Barney emerged from his terrifying experience intact and smelling fresh. On the way back to our apartment, Joshua stopped in his tracks. He looked up at me with a glint in his eyes and a mischievous smile on his face. It was a familiar look. I knew he was plotting something as he exclaimed,

I have an idea! Let's wash Barney again, only this time, I won't pray, and we will see what happens. Then we'll find out if there really is a God. While I was impressed with his pursuit of empirical evidence, I suggested we leave well enough alone, with some questions left unanswered.

When he lost his first baby tooth, he refused to believe our fantastic story about the tooth fairy. Determined to prove us wrong, he stayed awake until we tip-toed into his room to trade the tooth hidden under his pillow for a sack of coins. Instead, we were met with a flurry of activity and flash of light as he snapped a picture with a camera he hid under his pillow.

Aha, I knew it! He shouted out. While we delighted in his ingenuity and intelligence, we never doubted that Joshua was a little boy, albeit a kind and gentle boy. We were delighted that our son pursued his own interests without being constrained by gender-based social expectations. Roger and I wanted both our children to be nurturing, loving human beings, and to have the same opportunities to pursue their individual interests, regardless of their gender.

Joshua was perfectly content to wear jeans or overalls, except for the three piece corduroy suit he wore to his cousin's Bar Mitzvah. He would have worn it every day if we let him. Like most children, he had fun dressing up, but never in female clothing, not even for Halloween. Goofy, creative costumes, hats and wigs were more his style. Cars, trucks, building blocks, and computers were his preference, but he, like some of the other little boys in our neighborhood, was willing to play house and dolls with his sister and female playmates. He especially enjoyed play dates with a kindergarten friend, ironically named Jennifer. They played with Barbie dolls at her house, and trucks, puzzles, and building blocks at ours. Toy guns were deliberately absent from both of our homes.

Joshua was not at all interested in sports and neither were we. My sister, concerned about her nephew showing up at school after an important game without knowing who won, or even who played, often called in the morning to brief him. With an amused smile on his face, he graciously listened and thanked her for the information.

As a child, our daughter Sarah was as comfortable wearing frilly dresses or pink ballet outfits, as she was in overalls. She gravitated towards puzzles, books, and dolls, showing no interest in cars or trucks, yet today she is an automotive technician, owner of an auto repair shop, educator, and an inspiration to women of all ages. She was born female and is very comfortable being the woman she is, despite having to break down stereotypes in order to succeed in a profession almost completely dominated by men.

After Jenni's death, as we sifted through boxes of toys, we found Barbie's head on Ken's body. Naturally, we assumed Joshua did it years before coming out. What a good laugh we had when Sarah revealed she was the one who switched the heads, but with no particular motive or hidden meaning – just playing. To this day she enjoys taking things apart and putting them back together, not always as they were meant to be.

No one can change a child's self-identity, regardless of how they are dressed, what toys they are given, or what activities they are permitted to join. Gender identity - how one perceives oneself - is independent of anatomy and perceptions of parents, or society. For children whose bodies match their gender identity, the process of growing up seems relatively straightforward. For children whose bodies do not match their gender identity, however, growing up can be torturous in a society which dictates how people should dress and act based on their anatomy.

When Jenni first came out, it was painful to imagine what my child might have experienced in our society which draws clear distinctions between males and females. The first thing an infant hears upon entering the world outside the womb, or perhaps while still in the womb is *it's a boy,* or *it's a girl.* If the genitalia are ambiguous, the baby might be whisked away as the doctors decide to advise the anxious parents to raise the child as a boy, or as a girl, and lay out options for corrective surgery.

When the genitalia are clear, but inconsistent with identity, growing up must be extremely difficult. It is not easy for a child to contradict parents, teachers, friends, or even doctors who assign such children a category to which they do not belong. People naturally respond to what they see, a boy or girl, and it becomes increasingly more difficult to assert otherwise, especially when a female is born into a male body. Little boys who express an interest in wearing dresses are frowned upon, even if the preschool teacher says it is okay in dress-up corner. After a while it stops being acceptable, and the social cues regarding so-called cross-dressing might instill a sense of shame. To the child, it is dressing appropriately, but to society, it is not. Sensing this, children who are mismatched with their bodies often hide their true identities, becoming quite adept at denying who they are, even to themselves.

Once during bedtime rituals, Joshua looked up at me with his big round eyes and asked why he was different from other children. He might have been six or seven years old at the time. I wonder if this was an opening I missed at a time when Joshua was becoming more aware his body was not growing in the way he expected, or wished it would. I said he was different because he was such an intelligent little boy with interests most other children did not have. Had I asked what he meant, perhaps he would have revealed his confusion about his gender.

It was true however. He *was* different. And we, as doting parents, had him tested when he was in second grade. The psychologist reported that he was very highly gifted, off the charts at genius level. Nevertheless, school presented a challenge for him. Young in his grade, highly intelligent, and not athletic, he was often picked on by classmates and older children. Many years later, Jenni told us that in kindergarten, a few older children picked him up and put him into a bathroom sink. Typical of many children who are victimized, he did not tell anyone for fear of reprisals. Instead, he carefully avoided using public bathrooms, expressing instead distain for bodily functions as they interfered with his day.

At our very first parent- teacher conference, Joshua's kindergarten teacher said he must learn not to ask so many questions. When I was in elementary school, I too asked a lot of questions. Rather than give me more challenging work, my teachers kept me busy helping other children with their work, delivering notices around the school, or reading to younger children. The novelty quickly wore off, as I learned to stop caring about schoolwork, leaving me unprepared for the demands of high school and college. No one would stop my child from asking questions. Teach him to ask at appropriate times and provide such a time, but never tell him to stop asking.

Violin lessons, replaced later by piano, science and arts programs after school, weekends, and summer were not adequate to fill the void left by a school system which failed to sufficiently challenge my child. My mission was clear - change the system. As an advocate for enrichment programs through magnet school funding, I networked throughout the community in Queens where we lived, and throughout New York City, eventually gathering support to run for a seat on the local school board. It was an unsuccessful run as the system would not be changed in that place at that time. Fortunately we were able to move to a Montclair, a progressive community in New Jersey with an exemplary magnet school system.

The new school provided challenges which held Joshua's interest and satisfied his curiosity. Between third and fifth grades, he took classes in computer programming, conversational French, clothing construction, woodworking, and international cooking, all in addition to his regular academic program. For the most part it was a perfect fit.

One day, Joshua nearly flew off the school bus, anxious to tell me about the delicious chocolate bread he made in his cooking class. We absolutely had to make it again at home immediately, if not sooner. Amused by his enthusiasm, I agreed, even though the proportions on the rumpled handwritten recipe seemed a bit odd. His response to my questioning the recipe was emphatic and insistent. *I copied exactly what the teacher wrote on the blackboard. It is right, mommy! Really, it is!*

And so we went to work, mixing, kneading, waiting for the dough to rise, and finally putting the loaf we shaped into the oven. Sensing my skepticism, he assured me it would be delicious. Sure enough, the irresistible scent of fresh bread and chocolate filled the air, but alas, the finished product, as I had suspected, was rock hard and inedible. With a sheepish grin, he admitted he made up the recipe, having thought it would be a terrific idea to make chocolate bread. The next day, we found a more plausible recipe and tried again.

Joshua thrived academically in his new school, but again he was picked on and bullied. He complained of being punched, kicked, or scratched by classmates as he passed them in the hallway. Rather than join the other children in the lunchroom, he chose to eat lunch in the nurse's office, a safe haven during recess as well. As personable as he was at home with family and other children in the neighborhood, he did not fit in socially with the kids at school.

Teachers and principals listened sympathetically, shook their heads, and said there was nothing they could do when I reported my child was the target of hallway attacks. More than once we heard the same familiar refrain. *Kids will be kids. Boys will be boys.*

Pushing, shoving, name calling – it was all part of growing up, they said. This was the prevailing attitude in the early 1980s and sadly, that attitude persists today. I did not agree then, nor do I agree now. Purposefully harassing or hurting another child, or being hurt, is not a necessary developmental milestone. No child should ever be afraid to eat lunch in the lunchroom, play in the playground, or even go to school.

As delightful as Joshua was, we were concerned about his apparent difficulty in fitting in socially with his peers and we consulted mental health professionals who for the most part tended to blame the victim, suggesting that our child might in some way evoke bullying. I wonder if other children sensed that he was different, not like the other boys. Joshua never revealed angst about being a boy, and nobody even contemplated he was uncomfortable with his gender.

Sarah, how do you make friends? Joshua once asked his little sister.

I don't know, she replied, shrugging her little shoulders. *You just do.*

What came so easily and naturally to her, at five years old, was a mystery to him at nine. Thinking that participation in organized activities might help him fit in with his classmates, we enrolled Joshua in the little boys' soccer team in our neighborhood. Somewhat enthusiastic at first, the novelty of special shoes and a spiffy uniform quickly wore off. At his first game, we could see he was uncomfortable, not knowing what to do and not really interested, even when there was an opportunity to kick the ball. His lack of interest did nothing to endear him to his teammates, and we allowed him to quit the team as soon as he asked to do so. Cub scouts proved a better choice, with challenging activities and proficiencies to be met. But by the time he was ready to become a boy scout, he had lost interest in the increasingly more aggressive horseplay of his age-mates. A Saturday program for gifted and talented children offered at the local college was more to his liking, and he eagerly went off to the summer camp they offered. It was a good match and he got along well with the other children.

At the start of middle school, Joshua was beaten up in an unsupervised locker room. When he returned to school after recovering from his injuries, his sympathetic principal arranged for an older student to accompany him in the hallways. This provided some degree of protection, but we knew a change was necessary. Our child's safety took precedence over our unwavering commitment to public education, so we enrolled him in a small private school. Fortunately, he won a scholarship as tuition was well beyond our means. It was a perfect environment to develop social skills while meeting his intellectual needs. There he made friends with all the other children. Bullying was not tolerated in that environment. Instead, children were taught to respect and get along with one another.

After his private school experience, Joshua opted for the larger student population and diversity of our local public high school. Those middle school years in a small, nurturing environment, where children were kind and respectful to one another, gave him the confidence to broaden his social circles. Joshua made friends easily in high school, especially with his academically advanced and creative peers, and he participated in numerous school activities, mostly related to the arts. Outwardly, he appeared quite comfortable with himself, confident enough to express his uniqueness by growing a neat beard and allowing his hair to grow long.

As unique as I thought my child was, I knew there were other children who did not fit into the mainstream of school culture. At various times throughout his childhood, I became an advocate for gifted programs, positive school environments, and comprehensive reproductive health and family life education. With work and graduate school, serving on committees kept me very busy, sometimes too busy. Nothing changed radically, but change is slow. At least discussions were opened, sometimes about rather controversial topics, but never about transgender issues, which was off the radar at the time.

At one point during high school, Joshua experimented with alcohol, recording his reactions after each drink. I came home from work in time to find him sick and nearly unconscious. A trip by ambulance to the emergency room was chalked up to adolescent testing and pushing limits, yet I stayed home the next day to take

Joshua for a long walk in the park. I wanted to give him an opportunity to explain his motivation and to reinforce that his behavior was dangerous and unacceptable.

Years later, after Jenni came out to us, I wondered if she would have revealed her inner turmoil and questions about gender identity during her childhood and adolescence had we asked the right questions. She quickly disabused me of that notion saying that she never would have told anyone, not even doctors or counsellors we consulted at various times. The general consensus was he would outgrow the behaviors which caused us concern.

In the nineteen eighties, when Joshua was growing up, there was no context for children to question their gender identity. Jenni told me her searches for information in the library and calls to mental health hotlines were fruitless, leading to her decision to put away such questions, and accept himself as a boy, who would grow up to be a man. While his masculinity was never called into question, stereotypically male behaviors were not typically displayed in our household. Sarah once remarked that Joshua was not like her friend's older brothers who enjoyed teasing, horseplay, and other manifestations of testosterone surges. Instead, he seemed to her to be more like an older sister.

Joshua did indeed mature into a gentle and charming young man, keenly interested in learning as much as he could about everything, but most of all quantum physics and computer science. He wanted to contribute to the digital revolution that he hoped would lead to a time when everyone would have computer access to vast amounts of information and discussions about any topic. The world of technology offered a place where he felt comfortable hiding his true identity.

During high school, Joshua wrote a short science fiction novel which included hints of gender change. Transformer toys were popular at the time, and we thought nothing of a character changing from male to female and back again, especially given a context in which another character could transfer memories and personality into a computer program. The idea Joshua might have been expressing a desire to change his own gender never entered our minds, and he did nothing to connect the dots for us. His characters were just characters, and we made no attempt to identify him with his story. Looking back, it was plainly there for us to see.

Like her ancestors who sought a better life in a new land of new ideas, Jenni, or Joshua, whatever name we remember her by, knew there was far more to life than what she saw around her. Jenni imagined a world of possibilities for existence throughout eternity, outside the boundaries of the body, as an idea continuing through time. After graduating high school in 1991, Joshua went on to study computer engineering at Tufts University in Boston. During his first year, he became intrigued by the idea of memes and the possibilities for transmitting knowledge and ideas. *Of Man, Mind and Machine*, a paper he wrote for a class was posted on the Internet and included in numerous college curricula. A version of it, *The Memetic Web*, included in the appendix, was later published in the 1996 catalog of *Ars Electronica*, an international festival celebrating the arts, technology, and society. At the end of his freshman year, his interest in three-dimensional holographic representation and virtual reality led to a summer internship at the University of North Carolina, which had a state-of-the-art, super-computer laboratory.

Joshua could not wait to share what he learned when we visited him in Chapel Hill. First, he gave us a virtual tour of a museum on his computer screen as he enthusiastically discussed the potential for the Internet. Next, he led each of us, in turn, to another screen and handed us special gloves and goggles to wear. He instructed us to watch the video and move our hands to control the car on the screen in front of us. When it was my turn, I felt as if I was traveling in a car at top speed on a road that opened endlessly in front of me. The sensation of actually driving the car was very real. After a few virtual crashes, I learned how to move my gloved hand to control the vehicle and slow down to enjoy the scenery along the way. With a big grin and a twinkle in his eyes, Joshua talked about the possibilities for virtual reality in training and education for drivers and pilots. Next, we went to another screen.

Want to see something really neat?

Even more neat? What? I asked.

Yup! Mandelbrot sets!

Mandelbrot! Grandma Esther used to make Mandelbrot, I quipped, referring to the Eastern European version of biscotti, or twice baked cookies.

No, not that – come check this out, he said with a giggle as he grasped my hand.

On the computer screen in front of me, an intricate paisley-like design continually open up from random points on the screen. Named for Benoit Mandelbrot, who was responsible for the development of fractal geometry, Mandelbrot Sets, or fractals, as they are commonly known, depict a complex mathematical formula. I was mesmerized by the colorful, self-replicating patterns. These patterns intrigued me and I wondered about the significance of new patterns emerging endlessly to infinity, yet the idea my son would one day become my daughter had never entered my mind. What I saw was a brilliant young man thrilled to be part of the revolution brought on by computer technology which was about to dramatically change the way we communicate and access information.

I can only imagine Jenni's excitement if she were alive today to witness the world of possibilities, expanding much like fractals to usher in Google, Google Earth, Wikipedia, Facebook, digital music files and digital photography, Skype or Facetime, touch screens, smart phones, 3D printing, and self-driving cars, none of which she experienced in her lifetime. This would have been her world had it not been interrupted by the unpredictability of when life ends and the future ceases to exist.

The idea of volume rendering, a technique for displaying a three-dimensional representation of two dimensional data, intrigued him and he wrote computer code to transform, in real time, digital data from an MRI (Magnetic Resonance Image) or Sonogram into a three-dimensional hologram. The world of software development was accelerating at an ever increasing rate, yet the ability to perform such volume rendering in real time on a laptop computer represented a tremendous breakthrough at the time. Anxious to further develop and market his program, he wanted to leave college to start a business, but we insisted he continue his studies.

We finally relented and allowed him to quit mid-way through his sophomore year following a pattern established in the computer industry by the likes of Bill Gates and Steven Jobs, both of whom had quit college to start Microsoft and Apple Computers, respectively. After careful consideration and consultations with friends, we decided to support Joshua in pursuing his goal. We helped him settle into an apartment and office space near Boston. There he launched *Lateiner Dataspace Corporation* to further develop and market his software program, which he named *Vox-L*. At nineteen, our son managed an office, hired software engineers to help with the project, designed marketing brochures, wrote articles, and secured speaking engagements at conferences and conventions. An article he co-authored demonstrating the potential of his software as a diagnostic tool was published in the *Journal of Radiology,* which led to invitations to present his program at various medical conferences. Along with the team he assembled who shared his vision, Joshua worked tirelessly to further develop his software, traveling around the country, speaking to groups of physicians and hospital administrators, and to other software companies.

When invited to set up a booth at Comdex, a large computer show held annually in Las Vegas, Nevada, Joshua asked Roger and me to help demonstrate his software, but requested we remain anonymous. He wanted to appear not only independent of his parents, but much older than he was, thinking this tactic would give him more credibility. It was a difficult task for us as parents swelling with pride at the accomplishments of their son. Nonetheless, we managed to keep secret our real identities to comply with his wishes. As company sales associates using assumed names, we demonstrated the *Vox-L* software's capability to visualize in three dimensions an MRI generated image of a brain, noting it was being done in real time on a laptop. Using an on-screen slicing tool, we could move and rotate the image, cut into it to view slices taken from any angle. I particularly enjoyed turning the head to look down from the top, then slicing progressively deeper to expose the mouth and teeth. These innovative demonstrations attracted large crowds and we were very busy each day of the conference.

Despite the recognition Joshua enjoyed, potential customers were not yet ready for a program using Windows based technology, which was very new. After three years, it was clear Joshua was way ahead of his time. He was unable to finance the business with sales of his software, and we could no longer afford to be his sole support. We decided it was time to close down the office, hoping he would further develop his product and sustain the business from our home.

Once, during his early teens, Joshua half serious and half joking, said, *Let me get this straight. You both work for nonprofit organizations. Why? How could you do this to me?*

We wished we had been able to do more and wondered what might have been had we been wealthier, more business savvy, and willing to take greater risks. Back and forth we bantered, asking ourselves, *what if?* When we expressed any hints of self-recrimination to Joshua, he insisted he did not blame us for the failure of the business. Rather, his spin was the experience he had gained would be invaluable as the rest of his life unfolded.

Joshua, about four years old

Middle
school
antics

Keys to
the family
car, 1990

Dressed for a
concert, 1988

Joshua and
Sarah, 1991

Our family,
Montclair, 1992

Demonstrating his software, 1994

June
1995

After
coming out,
Fall 1996

Jenni, Portland, 1996

Minneapolis, Winter 1997

California Girl, 1997

First visit home, Spring 1997

Sarah and Jenni, home for the holidays, December 1997

Our family with Margaret, San Francisco, March 1998

Muir
Woods,
March
1998

Margaret and Jenni

Days before the Accident

Karen Shiffman Lateiner

Chapter 14

Becoming Jenni

During the three years Joshua lived in Boston managing *Lateiner Dataspace, Inc.,* I made frequent trips for a weekend, or sometimes for a week, to help manage the office. Joshua was over his head in responsibility and stress had begun to take its toll, especially when it became apparent his dreams could not be realized. Joshua's vision for every doctor's office to be equipped with his software for visualizing digital MRI and sonogram data in three dimensions was too far ahead of the times.

I sensed something else going on besides the impending failure of the business. There may have been opportunities when he might have shared his secret about identifying as a woman, but instead we talked about everything else. I wondered if I had failed to read his cues well enough to ask the right questions, or elicit a more in-depth conversation. Alternately, Joshua may have become so accustomed to denying his true identity even he was unable to reveal it. Or, he may not have known how to come out to me, perhaps thinking he would disappoint me if he did. Nothing could have been further from the truth. Sensing something was troubling my child was far more disturbing and stressful.

As a teenager, Joshua enjoyed trying on different looks. We thought it nothing more than adolescent expression. Months after our return from a family trip to London, where young people in

Piccadilly Square showed off their brightly colored, spiked hair styles, Joshua called me at work to warn me I might be surprised when I saw his new haircut. He said that he had planned to trim his sideburns, but in the process of trying to make them even, he shaved just a bit too far. Trim he did, all the way up the sides of his head leaving a two-inch wide swath of hair from his forehead to his neck. Weeks later before heading off to a concert with friends, that strip of hair was colored bright red and waxed to stand straight up.

Not long after he let his hair grow long to fall naturally in dark, loose curls, except for a small strip he bleached light blonde. He kept this look throughout most of high school, which included an after-school job at a local law firm. In preparation for college interviews in his senior year, he cut his hair short, grew a beard, which he kept well-trimmed, and traded t-shirts for button- down shirts which he wore with black jeans or trousers. This more mature and professional look became the facade behind which Joshua kept his identity as Jenni well-hidden, in preparation for entering the world of adulthood as the man he was expected to become.

One weekend while I was staying with Joshua in Boston, he invited me to go to a dance club with him, not as his mom of course, but as a friend visiting from New York. Not one to go to clubs, I was curious and went along. As soon as we arrived, he settled me in at the bar, while he disappeared into the crowd. Before joining the other young people dancing to loud music, he took off his conservative sweater to reveal a rather wild costume constructed from a torn shirt held together with leather and chains. Joshua appeared to fit in well with the others who were similarly dressed. He spent the night dancing while I sat at the bar sipping soda, somewhat perplexed, but glad he was enjoying himself. Fortunately, the club closed early according to Boston's strict curfew. Everyone walked outside to mill around under the light of the street lamps. Joshua chatted with a small group of young people and exchanged business cards before they dispersed. Apparently many of them were involved in one aspect or another of the computer industry. What a stark contrast from the loud music, crazy outfits, and energetic dancing one minute to industrious reality the next!

When the time came to close down *Lateiner Dataspace,* or at least move it to a less costly location, which we thought might be our home, we helped Joshua pack up the office and his apartment. Joshua showed us two stunning photographs taken by a professional photographer. One depicted Joshua tearing at metal chains wrapped around his body. The other portrayed him in clown-like make-up wearing a forlorn expression. We thought they might reflect his state of mind as his struggled with shutting down the business. Never did we think it was a reflection of an inner turmoil to hide his true identity as a female. Looking back, the symbolism was clear.

Just before his twenty second birthday, after a few months of living at home, Joshua announced his decision to move to Portland to join his girlfriend, Kara, whom he had met in Boston. Apparently, the idea of setting up a home office in our finished basement was not as attractive to Joshua as it was to us. We sent him off with tears and hugs after filling his car with food for the long trip ahead. As requested, he called every evening to let us know he arrived safely at each destination along the way. During one conversation it sounded as if he were in pain. He reported that he bumped into a doorway and hurt his shoulder as he brought his bags into a motel for the night.

Unbeknownst to us at the time – we learned nearly a year later -- Joshua arrived at his girlfriend's doorstep in a skirt and a new hairdo with a request to be called Jen. Kara was taken completely by surprise, but did not turn him away. His male persona no longer viable, he was no longer able or willing to keep his identity hidden. In retrospect, I cannot help but wonder if somewhere in the middle of the country he encountered someone who did not like the way he looked dressed in a skirt. If this were the case, Jenni was lucky to get away with just a bruised shoulder. Transgender people continue to be at great risk for being harassed, bullied, beaten, and even murdered for expressing their true identities.

Still totally ignorant of what our child was experiencing in terms of his identity, we focused solely on his professional identity crisis as the source of uneasiness. He spoke with us on the phone, but it was clear he did not want to go into details about his life, except to say everything was fine and he was working things out. Between the lines, Roger and I both knew there was more. He seemed to be struggling, yet we wanted to give him space and time to be independent and explore options, reassuring ourselves he was level-headed and would find his way before long. We treated his move across the country as a gap year, a year of self-discovery, before deciding on the next steps he needed to take as an adult. Still, our conversations, while frequent, were unusually strained. I was very concerned.

I tried to mask my angst by turning it inward, forcing it to retreat, especially when asked how Joshua was doing. My responses were generally cheerful and positive, yet stress began to wreak havoc on my body. The same year, I underwent surgery for a hysterectomy following a hemorrhage from a benign fibroid tumor. I cannot help but wonder if my anxiety about the well-being of my child played a role. Emotions, secrets, and even identity cannot remain hidden forever. Seeking release, they disrupt the balance we all seek to maintain, sometimes causing physical or psychological distress.

Once settled in, our child, whom we still knew as Joshua, took a job at a local coffee shop, supporting himself on tips. It was not my habit to frequent coffee shops, but I found every opportunity to patronize our local coffee shop to leave an extra generous tip. As I added my contribution to the jar on the counter, I made a silent plea to parents of Portland to do the same for the young people working there. My friends joined me in sending silent messages to parents everywhere to tip generously to help all those young people working in coffee shops or restaurants while finding their way in life.

Meanwhile, across the country, our son Joshua was known as Jen, later Jennifer, or Jenni. All the while, Sarah knew what her brother was doing. Before leaving, he confided his plans to arrive in Portland in women's clothing, making her promise not to tell us. Sarah dutifully kept this secret I believe she barely understood herself, except perhaps as another one of Joshua's fantastic ideas to get attention. What a terrible burden it was for her, yet she complied, keeping his secret safe with her and away from us.

We always thought our children could freely discuss anything with us. Apparently, we were wrong. Jenni had to first come out to herself before coming out to her sister, and only later to us. Given the prejudices and lack of understanding pervasive in our society, especially at that time, it had to be difficult to come out, even to parents who are open minded and accepting, as we always thought we were. Nonetheless, the idea our son was transgender was furthest from our minds.

Throughout her young life, Sarah was an activist, rallying first for animal rights, later for women's rights, gay rights, and human rights. She marched in demonstrations in our home town, New York City, and Washington, D.C. In high school, she and two friends started a chapter of Gay/Straight Alliance (GSA), a program developed for high school students by a national organization known as the Gay, Lesbian and Straight Education Network (GLSEN). The purpose of the program was to educate students about gender diversity, provide a safe place for gay students to come out, and for straight students to learn about diversity and become allies rather than adversaries. While gender bending was prevalent at the time, being transgender, actually living as a member of the opposite sex, was barely recognized or discussed.

On prom night, Sarah wore a rented tuxedo and her date for the evening, a female classmate and friend, wore a gown. No one made a fuss in our liberal town even then in the mid-1990s. We applauded the statement she was making. However, I did wonder if she was trying to tell us something about herself. When I asked, she emphatically said she is quite happy being a girl, and is definitely attracted to boys. It is always heartbreaking to hear that a prom or other school activity is cancelled because a student might show up dressed in clothing inconsistent with his or her gender assignment at birth, or because a same sex couple might show up to enjoy the evening with their friends.

Meanwhile in Portland, unbeknownst to us, Jenni joined a support group for young adults struggling to understand their discomfort with their bodies. She started counseling and was diagnosed with Gender Identity Disorder. After living full time in gender consistent clothing and undergoing evaluation by medical and mental health professionals, Jenni's counselors and physicians agreed to support her in transitioning from male to female. She was given a prescription for hormones to suppress testosterone and feminize her body. For people who are transgender, coming out and starting this long process marks a huge milestone, providing more psychological relief than any of us can even begin to imagine.

Coincidently, when she started hormone treatment, we noticed a dramatic change in the tone our phone conversations. Our child sounded more relaxed when we spoke, and we were relieved thinking Joshua seemed to have found his way and would be fine. Roger, who had been troubled by Joshua's apparent inability to focus on practicalities during earlier phone contacts, remarked he had his son back, and he enjoyed more frequent conversations with him. Our anxieties began to dissipate and as far as we were concerned our son, our dear Joshua, was resolving his disappointments about the business and moving on to redefine himself. We had no idea he was redefining himself as a woman.

Over the next two years, after finally coming out to us, we gradually grew accustomed to seeing our child as a woman after shedding the façade she wore all her life to hide her true identity. *Jennifer. Jenni. Jen. Joshua. Josh.* Whatever name we use, this would always be the same brilliant person – exhilarated by life and learning. She could always make me laugh with her wit, or just by being silly. And there was her beautiful smile, reflecting her warmth, compassion, and love of all living things.

After her death, we purchased a bushel of daffodil bulbs to distribute to friends and family with a request that they be planted in Jenni's memory. Every year, these golden yellow daffodils, renamed *Jennidils* by a friend, break through the hard winter ground to make us smile, just as Jenni always did, reminding us of the continuity of life. Dear friends from Israel visited not long after Jenni died. They took home with them an acorn from our park and planted it in their garden, where it grew into a giant oak tree as a living memorial to our child. Life does indeed go on.

Still, at random times during the day, I wonder what Jenni would be like today, knowing that I will continue to wonder until I can no longer wonder about anything. Jenni loved children and wanted a family of her own. By now she might have achieved all her dreams. Roger summed up our child's life in a poem he read at the unveiling of the monument we erected at the cemetery where her ashes are buried.

Ashes and Ideas

A wonder came upon the world
A child.
One of but a few such special spirits
Whose wingéd thoughts
Soared to heights and depths
Dizzying to most of us.

Whose mind encompassed galaxies and eons
Whose heart encompassed all who would not hate.
Whose will could even alter nature's chosen path

Who gave to all about
And wished to give yet more
And had so much to give

And who has now been taken from us
As if we did not deserve to share a world
Enlightened by her presence

The mystery that struck
Down one so young and joyful
Will not yield to the science of our time
No cause prime or proximate
Can we read to learn
The moral to this tale

All we have left
Are ashes and ideas

—Roger Lateiner, 1999

Chapter 15

Looking Back at Coming Out

At the time Jenni came out to us, transgender issues were not discussed, nor were there transgender characters portrayed in films or television shows. There is a period of adjustment after being told that one's adult son is living as a woman and changing his body to match his identity. It is a process both for the person transitioning and for the family. It takes time.

A Piece of the Puzzle

A perfect child was born.
A boy! A man child to take his place amongst men,
The great men of the universe.
The trajectory was set.
Age perfected perfection.
A handsome, confident man emerged from the boy.

Yet, one stubborn piece refused to fit.
Growing and gnawing from the depths of denial
It demanded release.
Not matter how much pushing and prodding,
That piece refused to fit.

It burst out, destroying in its path
The image of the man.
Relentlessly insisting on a picture of a woman
That imperfect, ill-fitting piece systematically
Destroyed my picture of perfection.
I wanted it to go away.
It would not. It had to be embraced.

The woman emerged, born of imperfection,
Released as the essence of all that is good.
Freedom to be, freedom to express, freedom to live!
The perfect child reborn.

I learned about absolutes and in-betweens,
The worlds of possibility between life and death.
Perfect - Imperfect. Man - Woman.
All one.

—KSL, 1996

Before Jenni came out to us, we had arranged to meet in Los Angeles. Roger needed to be there for a national meeting of the Screen Actors Guild where he worked, and we were both invited to a family wedding in the same city. It had been a year since we saw Joshua. He arrived in jeans and a t-shirt with his hair long and bleached blonde on one side. The other side of his head was shaved. Gone were the conservative haircut and button down shirts from the last time we saw our child, then a young man headed across country to meet his girlfriend.

While Roger was meeting with colleagues, Joshua asked that we go back to our room after breakfast as he had something important to tell me. He revealed a life-long struggle with gender and proceeded to tell me he already started hormone treatments to become a woman. He said he always felt he was a woman, but tried to make those feelings go away. He searched for information, but there was none. He did not even know what questions to ask or what to say. He kept this struggle with his gender identity buried inside him. He told me he changed his name to Jennifer, but everyone called him *Jen*, or *Jenni*.

The room began spin. I felt sick to my stomach. Finally, I burst into tears. There was never a hint. I was in shock and heartbroken at the thought of my child having gone through childhood and adolescence wearing a mask to hide his identity. The whole thing was incongruous. Knowing nothing about Gender Identity Disorder, I wondered if he was suffering from a mental breakdown brought on by the demise of his business. My sobs were uncontrollable as I felt the loss of the child I knew, not knowing what the future would hold. I wanted to understand. I wanted this whole thing not to be true, but when I embraced my child, I felt the hard breasts of a young woman against my chest. I knew right then there was no turning back.

For the duration of the weekend, we agreed Jenni would remain undercover so to speak. She was not ready to come out to everyone at once. Neither was I. It had to be one person at a time, slowly and patiently, a process that takes time. Jenni asked to meet with Roger alone as well. As soon as he was free, they met for dinner, just the two of them. Sometimes it is easier to relate to one parent at a time. Afterwards, as far as I can recollect, Roger and I just held each other tight, took a deep breath, and resolved to do whatever we had to do. That evening the three of us attended dinner with family members gathered for the wedding the next day. Just as Jenni did for so many years, Roger and I wore a mask.

The next day our friend Joe, who lived in the area, met us for drinks in the lobby of our hotel. Before Roger was able to join us,

Joshua went off to place our order, leaving me alone with Joe, knowing I would confide in him as we had agreed. I hoped that he, as a gay man, might offer me some insights. As soon as he was out of earshot, Joe turned to me and asked if Joshua came out yet, assuming from his androgynous, somewhat feminine appearance that he was gay. I told him Joshua came out as a woman. My usually talkative friend was speechless, except to say he knew nothing about what it means to be transgender. This was new territory for all of us in 1996, even in the gay community. Later the same evening, Joe called Jenni to offer his friendship and support. He implored her to be patient with us, reassuring her of our undying love, as well as his friendship.

Jenni's support group friends in Portland made her promise to call after she came out to her parents to let them know she was safe. They were concerned that we might have committed her to a mental institution, or forced her into intensive therapy to change her mind. Sadly, this was Jenni's frame of reference based on the experiences of so many of the gender non-conforming people she met. As confused as we were, that thought did not cross our minds. Instead, we wanted to learn more and seek out professional advice to confirm that our child was truly transgender.

Nonetheless, it took time to comprehend the enormity of the fact my son was now a woman. Not always knowing what to say, or how to act, I found it difficult to enjoy our time together over the next few days. Not ready to suddenly be plunged into this new role as the mother of a transgender child, I wished I had been prepared and knew something, anything, about what it means to be transgender.

Just before we had left for California and unbeknownst to me, Sarah broke her silence and revealed to Roger that her brother was living in Portland as a woman. Not knowing how to deal with this information and preoccupied with his work, Roger eventually told me that he pushed it out of his head, rather than share this incomprehensible news with me. He had other things on his mind and remained silent about what he knew throughout the entire plane ride across the country. When I found out I had been left out of the family circle of trust, I felt betrayed and angry. Those precious days with Jenni might have been easier, less confusing, and happier if I had time to educate myself beforehand. I thought about secrets and the impact of keeping them stored away, but there was more important work to do – learn everything I could about Gender Identity Disorder and what it means to be transgender.

Jenni was patient with us as we learned to adjust our expectations and embrace the new reality of our son changing his body from male to female. Taking hormones represents a significant challenge not only for those close to the person who is transitioning, but to the transitioning person as well. It takes time for the body to adjust to the changes brought on by the introduction of estrogen and testosterone suppressing drugs. On the one hand, the person may experience a tremendous sense of relief knowing they are finally taking steps to relieve the anguish of living in the wrong body. On the other hand, emotional upheavals and mood swings occur as the body adjusts to the hormones, similar to those occurring during adolescence when hormones surge through the body changing it from child to adult. People in the process of transitioning often refer to this period as a second adolescence no matter what their age at the time of transition.

Pronouns were a different story. Unlike many other languages, English words are basically gender free, except in singular pronoun form when we use *he* or *she, him* or *her.* During Jenni's first visit home, Jenni and Sarah berated us when we inadvertently addressed either of them by their given names instead of the names they gave themselves. At least we did not have to switch pronouns for Sarah - she was quite content with her gender identity, but preferred a nickname she gave herself. Despite our best efforts, we made mistakes to the great disappointment of our offspring who discovered we were fallible human beings. I suggested we turn the tables and try a little role reversal.

Let's pretend that I am now a man, and that Dad is now a woman. From now on, refer to me as Roger, or Dad, and to Roger as Karen, or Mom, and please, always use the correct pronouns. And remember - never, ever make a mistake. Much to our delight, neither of our children could meet their own strict standards. Try as they might, they could not call me Dad, or Roger, Mom. Before long, laughter filled the air. All was forgiven.

Jenni flamboyantly experimented with her new found freedom to be a woman. The contrast between Joshua's conventional mode of dressing and Jenni's outrageous, colorful outfits, sometimes verging on ridiculous, was startling. Looking back, I have a better understanding of what might have been going on for her as she tried to impress everyone with the fact that she was indeed a woman. I still had so many questions, and remain ever grateful for her patience. Jenni took time to answer my questions and explain the steps of her journey, as she guided me through mine, clearly explaining what it was like for her to grow up as a boy.

This is what it would be like for you if you were in the wrong body. You, Karen, are a woman, and know you are a woman. When you're young, you watch your sister develop as a girl becoming a woman, and wonder why you are not the same. Instead, when you look in the mirror you see a penis and cannot understand why it is there. Everyone else seems to accept your body the way it is, and you learn to accept it as well, always wondering when your penis will disappear and you will grow breasts like the other girls. Dark hair appears on your face, your arms, your legs, and on your back. And on your chest, instead of the breasts you expect, more dark hair appears. Again, no one seems surprised, except you. So you learn to live with it, thinking there is something wrong with you if you even have such feelings or think such thoughts. You don't even know what questions to ask. Finally, you can live with it no longer. You have to do something.

* * * * *

Her explanation was helpful. Still, it was incongruous to me. My little boy never voiced any objection to being dressed in male clothing, nor did he indicate any desire or wish to be a girl. Jenni understood my confusion and urged me to reach out to other parents of transgender children. At first I was reluctant, still not ready to accept that my child was transgender, but Jenni insisted, and I thank her for that. Jenni made email introductions to the mother of a transgender person she knew. Weeks later I called and confided in this stranger that I was confused about my child's revelation. All she said was, *I know.*

I know. Those words of understanding, true understanding from someone, who was once in the same place, hold so much power. Power to comfort, establish a sense of connection, and share experience. Only a person who has had a similar experience can utter those words honestly, as I learned after Jenni's death. I expressed my fears and concerns. Over the course of many conversations and email exchanges, we talked about the dearth of available information about transgender issues, freely sharing what we each had learned. Through Mary, I met other parents. The email exchanges grew to include even more parents struggling to understand gender transition at a time when so little information was available.

In contrast to the situation today where transgender people are more visible in the media and vocal in demanding basic human rights, there were few resources for understanding gender change. Once, at a national conference on research in child development, I took some time to look through the many books displayed on tables outside the conference rooms, scanning each index for the words *transgender, transsexual,* or *gender identity disorder,* only to find a paragraph in one, a sentence or two in just a few others. For the most part, I found nothing to help me understand why my son needed to transform his body to become a woman. I began to understand Joshua's frustration at not finding answers to his own questions when he searched libraries and called help lines. In the context of a little boy who said little until he could speak in full sentences, I understood his decision to put his questions away until he could find answers for himself.

Chapter 16

Piecing It Together

Ironically, the day after Jenni's accident, I had been scheduled to meet my email friend Mary to give her my submission for an anthology of stories by parents of transgender children. My story was ready, but never submitted, nor was it ever published.

There are Many Ways to be a Human Being

We were excited about seeing our son for the first time in nearly a year since he moved three thousand miles away, across the country. We arranged to meet in California where we were staying for a long weekend. It was a surprise to see him dressed in casual unisex clothing, sporting blonde hair on one side of his head, the other side shaved. Nonetheless, we were thrilled to see him.

While my husband was busy at a conference, Joshua told me that he had been diagnosed with Gender Identity Disorder, explaining that he needed to begin the process of transforming his male body to match the woman he knew he was almost all his life. I had heard of Christine Jorgenson, whose transition from male to female was reported in the news in 1952. I never would have imagined my child to be so mismatched with his biological gender that the only way to live a normal life would be to actually change his body to match his inner self — her true self. It was something I never thought about as a possibility. There were no clues, but with a little revisionist history, a new lens to look at the past, there may have been some indications. Still, they were there only in the context of this new information that our 22 year-old son was becoming our daughter.

My world turned inside out and upside down. How do we do this? Children don't come with instructions. How will people react? What will they say? What will they think? What do I think? I didn't know. It was all a blur and I was confused. None of this fit into any of my expectations. How could my son, whose gentleness and sweetness never hinted at femininity, declare that he was always a woman?

I wept. The tears were for my child who now revealed this life-long struggle with identity, always trying to make the strange feelings go away, totally denying them, never even admitting them to himself. Surely he never would have revealed it to anyone else. It was heartbreaking to find out that my child had been dealing with such profound confusion about his gender identity on his own for so many years, without help or guidance. I felt helpless, ashamed that I was unaware of my child's inner turmoil. I wished I had known. I wished that I had been prepared to hear what I was hearing for the first time.

Growing up can be a painful experience in and of itself. Growing up as a highly intelligent child, who did not quite fit in with his age-mates, added more pain. With each passing year, Joshua seemed to become more and more comfortable with himself and his peers. We had been so pleased to see our son finally grow into himself as a young adult. We did not know of his decision to put those strange feelings into the deep recess of denial. The pain of not growing up to be the person you expect to be -- the gender you expect to grow into -- is unimaginable.

I wept for myself and for my family, wondering how my daughter would come to terms with the fact that her older brother was becoming her sister, an older sister who looked to her younger sibling as a model for being a female. I worried about how my child would function as a woman, when she was brought up to be a man. Would she be okay? Was she okay?

At first, we thought our son might have had a break with reality. He had moved across the country, often a good thing for a young adult to do, to separate from the family for a while, to find one's self before settling into grown up life. We kept in touch and talked frequently. As a mother, I was concerned, but had no idea at the time that all the while my son was finding himself to be a woman. It was a blur of cognitive dissonance. Past experience did not fit into present reality. At the airport, we said good-bye to our son, our lovely son whom we hadn't seen for many months, whom we knew we would never see again, as him. It would be the last time I would ever hold my dear son close to me. My heart was broken, and I was sick with worry.

But I knew what I had to do. I needed to learn everything I could about this diagnosis of gender dysphoria. Years of graduate school studying developmental psychology did not prepare me for this, but it did prepare me to do research. And that I did between the tears. For two months I searched libraries, bookstores, and the Internet hoping to find answers. I closed myself off from friends - I couldn't talk anyway. Tears would choke the words, as I continued to grieve the loss of my son and try to understand his need to change gender. I could tell no one, not friends, family, or neighbors. If I told, it would be true, and like my child, I wore a mask to hide my sorrow.

Jenni suggested I get in touch with the mother of a transgender friend and a transgender rights activist, a woman she told me about months before. Still, I couldn't. One day when I checked email, I found a message to her, copied to me from Jenni, introducing us. She responded with a lovely message. Still, I couldn't reply. A few days later I got up the courage to email to ask for her phone number. Calling would be easier. Telling in writing would make it real. I still entertained thoughts I would wake up from this dream. Finally, I called her. We talked. I felt as if a weight were lifted. My initial annoyance that Jenni took the liberty of reaching out for me turned to gratitude and respect for her wisdom in insisting I seek support from someone who truly knew what I was experiencing.

I decided to seek additional professional support in trying to understand what it means to be transgender, and to guide me in coping as a parent. I found a psychologist known for her work in the transgender community, but my inquiry to schedule an appointment was met with a rather curt reply. She said that she did not deal with parents, and had no referrals for me. I called my health insurance plan to request the name of a therapist who dealt with gender issues, preferably in New York City, the city of anonymity, rather than in the suburban town where we lived and *where I knew so many of the therapists. The psychologist they recommended stated up front that she worked with many gay and lesbian clients, but had no experience with someone who was transgender or the parent of a transgender person. She said she would be willing to go through this with me if wanted to give her a chance.*

Her response was honest and affirming. I shared everything I learned when we met weekly, sometimes twice a week. At one point she divulged that she tried to imagine what it would be like for her if her own son, who was the same age as mine, announced that he was transgender. As hard as she tried, she could not imagine seeing her son as a female, nor could she imagine what I was feeling as a mother. She went through it with me, as a therapist, as a mother herself, and as a peer, sharing my pain and supporting me through periods of confusion, anger, guilt, grief, sadness, and acceptance. Her compassion and desire to learn with me gave me strength to move forward.

One day in the supermarket, I watched as a young man engaged in a beautiful interaction with his infant child. It appeared as a magnificently choreographed dance --- new father and infant responding to one another with overwhelming love and connection. This was a dance my son would never have. I left the store in tears, realizing I had to finish mourning the loss of my son, as well as the loss of the hopes and dreams I had for him.

We always have to get to know our children as adults. They never quite turn out as we would have expected. That is the beauty and wonder of it all. We nurture and love our children as they grow to be independent adults planning for their own future. The process of acquainting ourselves with them as adults can be joyous and exciting. But to get to know the child you knew as a boy, growing to be a young man, and then becoming a young woman, now a daughter was too confusing.

Was my close relationship with my growing son, a relationship I had cherished, all a fraud? I felt betrayed. It was an awful feeling. Did I ever really know my child? How could I have, if he could never share his inner turmoil? My new daughter was taking her place as an adult woman without having gone through the stages of being a young girl. Did she learn everything she needed to know watching her younger sister grow from little girl to strong young woman? Could she be properly prepared without a solid foundation of a mother-daughter relationship? Or perhaps, we always had a mother-daughter relationship. I just did not know it.

Yet, still not totally convinced, and also wanting the very best guidance, I found a place to get a definitive diagnosis, a place to rule out fears that our son might have suffered a break from reality. Dr. Eli Coleman, the Director of the Program in Human Sexuality at the University of Minnesota Medical School, which had one of the largest and preeminent gender identity clinics in the country, agreed to see us. Jenni, as my child now insisted on being addressed, agreed to meet Roger and me in Minneapolis for an appointment in the middle of January.

On the way there, I hoped for a magic pill that would make my child's thoughts of changing gender go away. We arrived in frigid weather and awaited Jenni's arrival at the hotel. It was the first time seeing her dressed as a woman. With the temperature outside below zero, Jenni stepped off the airport shuttle wearing the same man's topcoat worn throughout high school, over a short skirt, lace blouse, fishnet stockings, and heels. With a deep breath, I looked past her clothing to smile and embrace my child.

After three days of testing, evaluation, and interviews, the results were clear. We were told that our child was perfectly fine with no sign of mental illness, but definitely a primary transsexual. The best way for her to lead a normal life would be to transition. We were told that the fact she could come out and come to terms with her gender dysphoria was a credit to us as parents - Jenni had a strong ego and was highly intelligent. We were advised to love and support our child as we always had, and from now on refer to her by the name she chose for herself - Jennifer, or Jenni.

At least we had an answer. Now we could breathe. We knew what it was, that Jenni was not suffering from a breakdown, and would be okay. Now there could be a plan, a course of action, and a map of sorts to follow for this unusual journey. When we began this trip, we had no idea where we were going, what to do, how to act, what to say. Now we knew, but we were still unsure of how we would manage our network of family and friends.

I began to share my secret with friends. Each time I told someone, it was an emotional ordeal. I had to explain and help them understand. There were so many questions. It was exhausting and sometimes I found myself mothering and nurturing those who had a hard time accepting what I divulged. I needed them to understand and accept my child for who she was. The first time was with a friend who lived nearby and who had sensed that something was bothering me over the past months. We talked for a long time. I told her all I had learned about gender dysphoria. She listened and wanted to know how she could be supportive to me. I knew I could count on her. I shared my first coming out experience with my younger daughter, who had already begun to tell her friends. She said, "See mom, it does feel better to tell people." She was right. But it was still difficult - each conversation a long, emotionally draining process.

A cousin, a gay rights activist in whom I confided early on, said she thought my mother, who was very close to my son, but no longer alive, would be very understanding and accepting. I wore those words like a security blanket. We never stop seeking support and approval from our parents. That blanket shielded me from thoughts of relief my mother did not live to see this, thoughts suggested by others. Instead, I looked to the memory of my mother as a model for how to act and what to do. I know she would have embraced Jenni with all the love she showered on him as a child.

After a few months, Jenni came home for a visit. I had to let people know that the precocious little boy that everyone in our neighborhood and within our circle of friends and family knew as Joshua would be coming home as a young woman named Jenni. Reactions were interesting. One friend listened with understanding and concern. She immediately connected on the fact that growing up must have been such a painful process and wanted Jenni to know that she had a place to call home, with neighbors who would always love and accept her. This was in stark contrast to the reaction of a few others who made it clear they were not ready to see Jenni.

Another friend, a clinical psychologist, reached out to empathize, acknowledging how difficult this must be for us. She then suggested that perhaps we should not be supportive of the transition, as many psychotherapists felt that, with the right kind of talk therapy, a person with gender dysphoria might abandon thoughts of changing gender. Someone else, a physician, suggested we make our child come home, get him off hormones, and force him into therapy. Despite my relative ignorance at the time, this well-meaning advice did not feel right, even though it reflected the current state of common understanding in much of the professional community.

For the most part however, family and friends listened with understanding and empathy reminding us that above all our child was healthy and able to express her true self. They welcomed Jenni with open arms and were a great support. A friend's mother with the wisdom of her years said simply, "There are many ways to be a human being."

Yes, there are many ways to be a human being. We lost a son, but we did not lose our child. She is still the same person, still our child, still part of our family. As we adapted to this new reality, we read that the son of a celebrity was fatally shot on a California highway. That family truly lost a son, putting our loss into perspective as we imagined their grief to be unbearable.

I learned to look at life as a continuum of continuums. Even those first pronouncements of the delivering doctor, it's a boy, or it's a girl, are not always certain or clear-cut. Some boys are very masculine - some, not so much. Some girls are very feminine - some more like boys. All children, all people fall somewhere on the continuum from male to female. Just as there is a continuum of biological sex, there is also a continuum of gender identity. Where one falls on the continuum does not always match their physiological reality. Most males identify themselves as males. Most females identify as females. The gender identity of a transgender person, however, is diametrically opposed to their biological body.

Like a butterfly trapped in a cocoon, our child was forced to grow up confined in the wrong body. Only by coming out, coming to terms with her discomfort at being in the wrong body, and then taking steps to alleviate it by changing her body to match her identity, could she emerge as the woman she always was. Only then could she be free to express herself as a woman.

In the beginning, I mourned the loss of my dear son. After some time, my grief turned to acceptance of the daughter my child always was. I leave the pictures of Joshua on the piano. Slowly I add the new ones of Jenni. The past doesn't go away. I look at those pictures of my little boy and wonder what he was thinking, sometimes seeing the secrets in his eyes. We can remember, but now must accept the change.

Having a transgender child is not a tragedy. Losing a child is. We did not lose our child. No matter what, she remains our child -- the child we nurtured and will always love - the person who had the courage to come to terms with the biological mistake that tormented her for so many years. No, it is not a tragedy, but an event to rejoice, as one might rejoice in the metamorphosis of a butterfly, or of anyone finally able to be the person they truly are. It took time and a lot of work to come to this place of understanding and acceptance. To say it was easy would be untrue. It was not. I struggled with relationships, with pronouns, with very deep emotions. But the overriding feeling was that no matter how old our children, no matter how different they are from our expectations, they would never lose our love and support. My husband and I gave them a foundation to become themselves. We can watch the process, but we cannot change who they are.

Our family was transformed, in a way I never could have imagined. Our son was now a daughter. Our youngest child, the first daughter in the family, the first granddaughter, now had an older sister, who was once her older brother. Any transformation within the family has a profound effect on every member, even if unspoken or unacknowledged. Births, illness, death, marriage, divorce, moving - all these events introduce change into the family, sometimes very powerfully and profoundly. We deal with these changes in many ways -- sometimes in a healthy and constructive manner and sometimes not. Yet we adjust. We transform ourselves and our expectations.

Not a day goes by that I am not grateful that my child survived this process of coming to terms with her identity. It had been difficult, for sure. The process is grueling, arduous, and painful. Learning all I could about transgender issues and reaching out to people helped a great deal. Keeping a sense of humor and a healthy perspective on the true values in life kept me going. Our lives changed in a way we never would have imagined. I always considered myself to be open minded, but this experience opened my mind in a very powerful way that permeates many aspects of my life.

I still struggle with telling other people. I want to be in control of who knows and who doesn't know. Some friends have suggested that it might be easier for me if they tell others. In some cases that might be true, but I continue to be hurt every time I hear who has found out from whom. Just as it is not my place to announce which of my friend's children are gay or straight, I trust that my friends will show the same consideration. But news does spread - not in a malicious way, but merely as a point of interest. I have to wonder though, why friends who are curious about what they may have heard never reached out directly, instead making inquiries of other friends. For my own piece of mind, I try to believe that people are not gossiping but merely reflecting on the interesting events that occur in life. I'm still not sure. There are no guideposts for this part of the excursion, which is merely a side trip.

It took time, but finally I arrived at a place of peace and understanding. I am able to put Jenni's transition into perspective. My child is still my child and I can rejoice in witnessing her transformation. The future is yet uncharted, but I am confident that we will all find our way. It took many years for Jenni to come out to herself. It is understandable that it takes time for everyone to adjust to such a dramatic transformation of the family.

—KLS, May 1998

Chapter 17

Coping, as a Family, with Gender Change

After our meeting in Minneapolis, we had a few more days to be together before Jenni was scheduled to fly to San Francisco for an interview with Netscape, a computer software giant at the time. We wanted her to look her best and took her shopping for clothing. Roger helped Jenni choose skirts, blouses, and jackets. He waited patiently outside the dressing room while she tried on various outfits. Together they assessed what would be most fitting for the interview. I wanted to help, but found myself feeling helpless. It was too hard. Everything I picked out seemed right for Sarah, not for my son, even if now he was a woman. My reaction surprised me – I tried to be enthusiastic, but clearly I was not ready. Ashamed of my inability to help Jenni with her outfit, I retreated to let Roger take the lead, grateful he was there to help her. Roger later expressed to me, and to anyone who asked, that he so enjoyed being close to his child again. Gender did not matter in the least.

Whenever anyone asks how my husband coped with the change, I tell them the story of Roger helping his daughter, who was once his son, choose gender appropriate clothing. So often, it is assumed a father would have the hardest time accepting that his child was gay or transgender; yet another stereotype based on incorrect assumptions. We have since met many men who were open and loving to their gay or transgender children. And, of course, we met others who were not. It is so terribly sad to hear of parents who cannot accept their children and do everything to put obstacles in their paths.

From the time Jenni came out to the time she died, we all learned as much as we could and reached out to educate others. During her first year at Oberlin College, Sarah worked with friends and faculty members to organize a program about transgender issues. *Transgender Week,* the first event of its kind on a college campus, featured guest speakers and workshops designed to open dialogs and educate students and faculty about gender diversity. It was a huge success. Sarah invited Jenni to attend the following year if another such event were planned. Jenni enthusiastically agreed, but her death thwarted those plans.

Sarah had put us in touch with the sponsors of a support group for transgender people and their families in Cleveland. They themselves were the parents of a transgender adult child. Along with a few other parents of transgender children, we stayed in touch via email, sharing information, thoughts and concerns, relieved to know that none of us were alone. Word spread about this network of parents which quickly grew nationally, later internationally, to become a life-line of support and education for parents of transgender children, as well as for transgender and questioning youth and adults.

Through this network, I was invited to attend a *True Spirit Conference* and take part on a panel entitled, *The Care and Feeding of Squeamish Parents.* For security purposes, only upon registering was one privy to the exact location of the conference. It would have been too risky, given the prejudices at the time. Having never met anyone else who was transgender, except Jenni, of course, I had no idea what to expect. At first, there was the natural impulse to wonder if the person here, or over there, was always male, or always female.

Within minutes, my curiosity dissipated with each person I met and each story I heard. Gender, past or present, ceased to matter. Some of the people had undergone various surgeries to correct their bodies to match their gender identity, while others merely dressed in clothing to match their identity, all the time, or just some of the time. Each person was unique, adapting to their identity in their own ways, and in their own time. Some were embraced by their families, but most had been rejected, some even court ordered never to see their families or children again.

The experience of spending a weekend with hundreds of transgender men and women - female to male, male to female – was overwhelming and powerful. Some brought spouses, or significant others who were coping with their partner's transition. One can only imagine the dilemma faced by couples, gay or straight, if one partner comes out as transgender. If the relationship survives, the couple transforms to appear either heterosexual, or as a same sex couple, often facing rejection by their prior community of peers. Whether gay or straight, transition to the opposite sex often, but not always, results in familial and social ties being severed. At that time, transgender people were neither understood, nor accepted, even within gay and lesbian communities.

I spoke with many people and heard about their struggles with identity, beginning in childhood and denied into adulthood, sometimes late into adulthood. I learned that many transgender people, rather than come out to themselves or their families, live as they are expected, some marrying and having children. Some masked their inner turmoil with drugs or alcohol, eventually falling into depression, complete with suicide attempts. Tragically, far too many of these attempts are successful. We may never know how many suicides stem from severe depression because of the inability to express one's true identity.

A few years after Jenni's death, we learned of another set of grieving parents, whom we eventually met. They found their fourteen-year-old daughter's body hanging in a closet. Their child left a note saying she could not take being bullied at school for being a tomboy, when she truly was a boy inside, a secret she had kept hidden. Her parents never knew, and never suspected that being a tomboy was covering her gender identity as a boy. They wished they had known, and wished they could have done something to prevent their child from thinking that suicide was the only choice. Unfortunately, their story is not unique. There are too many stories of young people taking their own lives because of bullying, or because they are not accepted as they are, or who they wish to be.

Many teens, upon coming out about their gender identity or sexual orientation, are kicked out of their homes or forced into therapy, some of which can be harmful. Some run away from abusive situations, often to urban areas where they imagine they will fit in. Finding few resources even in big cities, far too many of these children are victimized by people taking the opportunity to exploit them. Drug dealing or prostitution are often the only means of survival in a society that marginalizes people who are gay or transgender, and makes it difficult, or impossible to find conventional employment. Sadly, drug abuse and sexually transmitted disease become by products of a society that can be rejecting and unyielding.

At the panel discussion the next day, all I could say to the group gathered was that it takes time to come out to oneself and time for parents to understand and adjust. My contribution, from the viewpoint of a parent, was to suggest patience when coming out to family, and refrain from slamming doors, or running away at the first sign of rejection. Nonetheless, personal safety has to be paramount. *Share your thoughts, struggles, questions, and provide information. Talk about how you feel, and what you have learned about yourself. It took years to come out to yourselves. Give your family a few days, weeks, or months, at the very least.* Perhaps somewhat innocently, I truly believed, or at least wanted to believe that with knowledge and support, the love of parents and grandparents would override the impulse to reject their child because he or she did not fit their expectations.

My heart ached for each person I met at the conference and for all the young people struggling to survive in a world that could not accept them as individuals or even try to understand them. I wanted to shout out that transgender and gay and lesbian people are beautiful, courageous human beings who deserve to be accepted by society, respected, rather than scorned, and afforded the same rights as anyone else.

When I returned home, I called Jenni to share what I had learned and to thank her for having been so patient with us. This was a journey of a thousand steps, each one bringing me closer to understanding, each one motivating me to learn and to educate people about transgender issues. I suggested we all go to the *True Spirit* Conference to be held the following year. Jenni liked the idea and we agreed that we would.

The next year, Roger and I did attend, this time to stand before the assembled group to tell them that our plans to attend the conference with Jenni were thwarted by her death. I told them all about Jenni – who she was and what it was like when she came out to us, and how she lived her brief life. I thanked everyone for sharing their stories the previous year and teaching me so much of what I needed to understand. Mostly, I needed them to know that because of their bravery in coming out and telling their stories, they were helping others see gender diversity is just another aspect of human diversity. When we left, I felt privileged to share Jenni's story, knowing her spirit would remain alive for many of those gathered.

Karen Shiffman Lateiner

Chapter 18

Emotional Roller Coaster

As a child, Joshua thought of the kitchen with all of its interesting gadgets and appliances as a playground or science lab. To him, the microwave could be used to dry clothing and the blender for concoctions both edible and non-edible. The salad spinner, a favorite, served as a centrifuge, or as a launch pad. When caught in the act, I dutifully reprimanded him, always with the same admonition, and a smile - *kitchen utensils and appliances for food preparation only!*

When Jenni came home to visit the last time, a stunning twenty four year old woman sporting short blond hair, she teased me with the salad spinner, spinning it around and around, reminding me of her childish antics. We laughed and repeated the familiar phase together - *kitchen utensils and appliances for food preparation only!* Two or three years after Jenni's death, Roger and I shopped for a new salad spinner in a local department store. Images of Joshua as a child and the glint in Jenni's eyes that last time she played with our old spinner clouded our minds and we were overcome with emotion. We ran out of the store and rushed into our car where we released a long volley of sobs. This was not the first, nor was it the last time that our emotions spilled out unexpectedly, often at the oddest times.

Yet I always welcomed the opportunity to talk about Joshua, or about Jenni, to keep her spirit alive, or take the opportunity to educate about gender identity. Somehow, at those times I was able to hold it together and not let my emotions overtake me. Friends, acquaintances, new and old – it did not matter. It was important to tell as many people as possible. I continued to write, but only during writing workshops. Writing what I felt at the time, sharing what I wrote in a circle of warm, supportive friends was my therapy.

Last Human Contact

Did she feel the warmth of the last human contact before her body would cease to exist as a repository for her spirit? Her spirit left her. Witnesses saw it as it released itself from the wreckage to become part of the universe - a universe that knew her and could be entrusted with her soul. As her body would disintegrate, her spirit, her soul, her life-force would live on forever. It is all that is left. We, the living, are entrusted to keep her spirit alive by remembering and telling her story. Jenni lives on through us and through those who remember her. For me, the retelling gives her eternal life.

I am reminded of the annual retelling of the Passover story of liberation from slavery in Egypt after the angel of death passed over and spared the lives of the first born sons of the Hebrews. Unable to protect my child from death, I can and will protect her memory and keep her spirit alive by telling her story.

—KSL, March 10, 1999

A friend once asked if I felt guilty. *Guilty? About what?* That I was unable to protect her from suffering, or save her from an untimely death? That we did not recognize Joshua's struggles with identity when he worked so hard to keep it from himself? I told her that I was experiencing so many emotions, a full range of emotions. Venturing down the road of guilt was not an option I wanted to explore. It is difficult enough to mourn, but to layer guilt on top of it would be unbearable. Surely, I have said, or done things that I might have done differently, but who could tell if any of these things would have changed the reality of Jenni's identity, or her death. I did the best I could with the information I had at the time. It is all any of us can do, without a window into the future. Of course, I wish there had been something I might have done differently to protect my child. Ultimately, it is the universal hope of mothers to keep their children from harm.

In the months and years following Jenni's death, I surrounded myself with positive nurturing people, friends and family who were always there for us with love and support. I could not tolerate being around anyone who complained about their children or expressed disappointment in them. For the most part, friends would stop themselves from issuing any complaints about their child when they remembered that mine was dead. A few would thoughtlessly go on and on about their son or daughter who is not thoughtful enough, studying the wrong subjects, working in the wrong job, wasting time, dating someone of another religion, is lesbian or gay, or any number of things parents might find to criticize about their children. Generally, I kept silent, allowed the person to vent, or merely said that ultimately everyone must make their own way and choose their own path. To the chronic complainers, I wanted to take them by the shoulders, look them straight in the eye, and say,

Your child is alive! My child is dead. I would do anything to have her back. Think about your complaints. How important are they? We

need to love our children, accept them, and appreciate their very existence, even if they do not meet our expectations, or hopes, or dreams. What you are telling me is not a big deal. Death is a big deal.

I wanted to take them to a meeting of parents whose children are dead, the club no one wants to join. There they would see a roomful of parents whose only complaint about their child is that he or she is dead. Who their children were, how old they were, what they did, and how they died no longer matters. The reality of death changes everything. These conversations often left me in tears, feeling powerless to communicate how precious life is. It seemed to me that only parents who have lost a child could truly understand that part of the experience.

My daughter Sarah once remarked that Jenni became perfect the day she died, an understandable observation from a younger sibling. We tend to exalt the dead, remembering only the positive, ignoring, and even forgetting, anything else that makes us human. With the passage of time I was able to talk about the excessive attention Joshua had received as a child because of his brilliant mind, his captivating, if sometimes annoying personality, and the ability to make me laugh at times when I might have been angry. Joshua was a tough act to follow for any younger sibling, and no matter how much we tried not to show favoritism, it was perceived, and my attempts to deny it were in vain. It makes me sad to think that before her twenty-first birthday, Sarah experienced the death of three grandparents, and her only sibling. Yet she emerged as one of the most capable and accomplished people I know.

Making sense of life, or at least trying to make sense of it, is part of each person's personal journey. Now an accomplished woman who is following her dreams and charting her own path, I believe that Sarah has incorporated Jenni's spirit into her own life. Jenni will be with her always, impacting her in ways not yet imagined. Occasionally we share stories – some evoke tears, while others make us laugh. One afternoon, years after Jenni's death, Sarah and I stared in disbelief as a thin, blonde woman dressed in black bicycled past our car, while we stopped at a traffic light. Simultaneously, we both exclaimed, *Jenni?* How ironic it was that this stranger looked like the older Jenni of our imaginations.

Sometimes a feeling of overwhelming sadness descends upon me like a veil interrupting those precious times I spend with Sarah, times I realize I will never have with Jenni. I wish I could say this goes away with time, but it just happens less often, as I learn to live with the reality of Jenni's death. Nonetheless, these fleeting nostalgic moments never undermine how grateful I am for every moment I have with my daughter, talking, laughing, doing things, or just being together.

There were days during the weeks and months, maybe even the first few years following Jenni's death when I wanted to stay in bed all day, pull the covers over my head and allow my body to sink into the mattress. I imagined staying there for days or weeks, magically thinking that I might emerge refreshed, and that Jenni's death was just a bad dream. Instead, the alarm would ring, but my body was too heavy to move from under the warmth of the covers. Occasionally, I would give in and linger, allowing myself to sink deeper and deeper. As comforting as it felt, it also frightened me, and I feared falling into a depression, or a deep despair. On those days I could almost hear Joshua's voice calling to me, from the edge of the Grand Canyon trail, as I struggled to climb those last few hundred feet. *Come on Mommy, you can do it. Come on Karen*, I would tell myself aloud. *You can do it.*

So, I would get up out of bed every morning to go to work, spend time with family and friends, and find ways to avoid a dreaded abyss of sadness and grief. I forced myself to walk - walking with friends was a lifeline – and I was fortunate to have both a park and friends close-by. The park was designed in the early post-Victorian era, when our community was first developed. Today a giant

Weeping Willow tree planted in memory of our child provides both shade and a place for children to play hide and seek. The idea that people of all ages and all walks of life, walked along these paths - conversing, laughing, sharing secrets, and expressing deep emotions - captured my imagination. Oh, if only the trees could talk - what tales they could tell! Walks in nature centered me. No matter where I was, Jenni's spirit surrounded me as part of the universe, the universe I knew existed out from under my bedcovers. I needed to breathe fresh air to feel Jenni's spirit. I still do.

Not long after Jenni's death, Sarah and I spent a weekend at a yoga retreat. I felt privileged for the opportunity to experience a series of workshops with my daughter. In one, we meditated, reflected, and wrote. In a room filled with strangers, lit only by sunlight and a single candle, we shared our private thoughts with the others in the room. Soon, I was enveloped in a cloud of stillness and comforting memories. I reached a place where I was finally able to balance my grief, integrate it into my existence as a part of me, just as Jenni's spirit was a part of me, along with the life-force of family, friends, and nature. It was this philosophy, such as it was, that allowed me to move forward, go back to work, and back to my life, which would never be the same.

Meditation Musings

Images through eyes slit open far enough
To contain the flame of a candle.
Struggling to keep other images from bombarding.
Stay with the flame. Breathe.
A road cutting through dense forest comes into view.
Winter drive through mountains and valleys.
Majestic pine forests dense and dark.
White barked birch, one after the other,

Letting in specks of light.
Images of color, of shape, of form,
Of outline against the sky.

The play of light in the morning, afternoon and evening,
Each a magical splash of surreal and eerie effects.
Bold straight sticks reaching skyward,
Defying the contours of the earth,
Each one perfectly parallel to the other.
Foliage reduced to an afterglow image in the morning light
Barely discernible -- a translucent textured fog.
How insignificant we are in the midst of these giant trees
Bursting out of every bit of unpaved earth,
Crevices in massive boulders,
Cracks in concrete poured years before
To hold back the force of nature.
The life-force of the earth, splendid, magnificent,
Words do no justice—
Just the images of colors, light and dark
Juxtaposed against the eternal sky.

As a child, a teen, and young adult,
I noticed the trees, the bushes, the flowers,
But only as part of a far more intriguing urban landscape.
Nature was. It was there. Pretty.
Pleasing to the eye.
Its pull not strong enough for my senses to linger.
It was just there.
Until I met the guy in the trees.
That's what my boyfriend thought I said
From a hammock hung between giant trees

Heavy with leaves against a moonlight sky.
No. The sky and the trees!
The silhouette of shapes captured me.
I took it in, absorbed it.
It took hold of me, and would not let go.
I had to fix my gaze.

It was a night of revelation,
Of form, of shapes, of light and dark.
Since that moment, almost thirty years ago,
I am held captive when I pause
To look up at the sky and the trees.
Each time a new experience, a never repeating pattern,
Even the same trees in a familiar sky appear new.
The sky and the trees, this guy in the trees,
Forces me to pause – makes me look
Not for just a moment, but really look.
See what is out there.
I want to capture the image, but I know it would be futile.
No artist, no photographer can recreate those images.
How could I even imagine I could?
It is only an image of a moment, like performance art.
It is when it is, not before, not after, eluding capture,
Defying containment on a canvas, or a photographer's lens.
But for all the defiance, the images of sky and trees
Forever accessible to those who linger
Allowing themselves to be captured.

–KSL, January 1999

Over the years since Jenni's death, I prefer being in natural environments, even if only passing by in a car. In those places where trees and mountains meet the sky, Jenni's spirit seems to permeate the air and I can almost feel her presence. I can never change the fact that life itself is transient, any more than I can bring Jenni back to life. Yet, each time I tell her story, or feel her presence, my sadness is balanced by the joy of knowing Jenni's spirit lives on.

Karen Shiffman Lateiner

Chapter 19

Diverting Grief

Acknowledging her previous male personae, Jenni asked me not to remove her childhood photographs, even when she brought her girlfriend home from California to meet us. She wanted her future fiancé to know everything about her. After her death, people close to us wanted to make donations in her memory. Jenni once told us that she wanted to donate money to the program in Portland where she received help in her transition. With her thoughts in mind, we set up a fund which we named the Jenni-Josh Lateiner Memorial Fund, acknowledging that Jenni was known as Joshua for most of her brief life. This fund enables us to provide support to programs for transgender youth, including those meant to prevent bullying.

Jenni's transition and the tragedy of her death opened many dialogs in our community about transgender issues. People genuinely wanted to know more. Not long after Jenni's death, we helped sponsor screenings at our local high school of *Youth Out Loud!*, a documentary produced by Sun & Moon Vision Productions, about the challenges faced by gay, lesbian, and transgender youth. After each classroom screening, the producers, whom we brought in from California, led small group discussions with students and teachers. *Youth Out Loud!* was shown again in the evening to the general public. Many of the students who saw the film during the day returned with their parents for another viewing along with a question and answer session. The program was very well attended by members of the school community as well as the community at large.

We hoped that screening would lead to others and it did. One was held at a local university, and another as part of a series of workshops organized at our local library fulfilling their mission to provide educational programming. Roger and I showed the film and told Jenni's story during one segment of the *Transgender Stories, Transgender Lives* series. Years later, I met someone, who told me that our story, as well as others he heard that night gave him the courage to finally become the man he was meant to be. Nothing could have been more gratifying.

As years went by, more and more information about transgender issues became available, yet libraries still lagged behind. Through the Jenni-Josh Lateiner Memorial Fund, we endowed our local library in Montclair with a collection of books and multi-media resources focusing on understanding human diversity, particularly on sexual minorities who are so often marginalized in our society. Bullying, discrimination, and hate crimes are an awful reality for anyone who is different, especially if they are gender non-conforming. Going to school can be a stressful experience for any child who is perceived as different, or not fitting in. We wanted parents, teachers, and children to have resources to better understand gender diversity and learn strategies to deal with bullying.

Every item in the Jenni-Josh Collection bears a bookplate depicting Jenni dancing on the beach framed by trees. Underneath is written, *Stay True to Yourself,* words Joshua wrote in a letter to the future placed in a time capsule and buried as part of his high school graduation ceremony. The time capsule was opened ten years later, three years after Jenni's death. With tears and hugs, classmates presented us with his letter. Realistic, or prescient, we will never know.

> *To the Future,*
> *I may or not be alive when this is opened. If I am alive, I have many hopes and aspirations for what I will have become. However, more important than who I am – I hope I will always be myself. Stay true to yourself.*
>
> *—Peace, Joshua. 6/26/91*

Meanwhile, in my professional life working as a mental health clinician at the University of Medicine and Dentistry of New Jersey, I took every opportunity to share what I had learned about transgender issues. When a call for volunteers to serve on a task force on gay and lesbian issues arrived in my inbox at work, I eagerly signed up. At the first meeting of administrators, faculty, staff, and students, I suggested that transgender issues be included in our mission. Subsequently a small sub-committee was formed to address the needs of the transgender community, that was, for the most part, underground at the time. Our objective was to provide a safe, bias-free environment where transgender members of the university and surrounding community could seek vital medical, dental, or psychological services. To increase awareness of the needs of this small, but marginalized community, we proposed educational programs for faculty, staff, and students. Our recommendations included access to gender free restroom facilities, and revision of forms for medical records to provide space for identifying as neither male nor female, but both depending upon point in time.

It was a good beginning that, at the very least, raised awareness within the university and planted seeds in the wider community. The

African American Office of Gay Concerns, tasked by the Department of Health to serve gay men with HIV/AIDS, expanded their services to reach out to transgender youth who, it was discovered, were living, for the most part, on the streets of Newark, NJ. These young people, some only fourteen years old, were invited to an event which included food, speakers, and swag bags filled with toiletries, make-up, and health related information, especially related to accessing medical and psychological services. This early outreach effort continues today with increased services for the local transgender community.

Although far from being an expert, I had learned a lot about transgender issues. Consequently, I was invited to speak to medical and psychology students. To my surprise, the idea of conceptualizing gender, gender identity, sexual orientation, perceived gender, and social role on independent continua was new to many of the students. Their education, not unlike that of most of us at the time, was constrained to think in terms of absolutes, male or female, gay or straight, with nothing in between.

To illustrate the notion that biological sex, gender identity, occupation, and sexual orientation are distinguished from each other, I would draw parallel, horizontal lines each representing different aspects of how we identify ourselves, and are identified by others, just as I did for friends and family who wanted to learn more about gender diversity.

Biological Sex	F--M	
Assigned Gender	F--M	
Gender Identity	F--M	
Sexual Orientation	F--M	
Occupation/		
Social Role	F--M	
Perceived Gender	F--M	
Perceived Sexual		
Orientation	F--M	

Using Jenni as an example, I would place a dot on each line to describe her as someone who was born biologically male and classified as male at birth. She identified as female, and was sexually attracted to females. She excelled in math and was a software developer at a time when the computer industry was even more male dominated than it is today. I placed a dot towards the masculine end of the line for occupation. Perceived gender well illustrated the temporal characteristics of how we appear to others. Before transitioning, Joshua was unmistakably perceived as a male. At the beginning of her transition, there may have been some ambiguity, thus the dot might be placed midway on the line for perceived gender. Over time the dot would move closer to the female end, ultimately reaching it in the eyes of most observers. Similarly, prior to transition, Jenni appeared to be a boy who was attracted to girls, thus perceived to be heterosexual. After transition, she remained attracted to women and appeared to be a lesbian.

I sometimes used another example, again drawing on my own family, saying I know a young woman who was born female, identifies as female, is perceived to be female, but who works in an almost exclusively male dominated field as an auto technician and educator. Despite what most people might assume, this person is attracted to the opposite sex, thus heterosexual. Other examples illustrated the need to break down stereotypes and recognize the potential for variations in gender and perceptions of gender, as well as the uniqueness of every individual.

Through the Department of Psychiatry where I worked, I had an opportunity to invite Dr. Eli Coleman, a world renowned expert on transgender health, to give a Grand Rounds presentation on gender diversity. I had met him when he evaluated Jenni at the Gender Identity Clinic in Minnesota and confirmed that transitioning was the best possible outcome for her. Included in his presentation was the fact that transgender people in various indigenous societies throughout the world were accepted in society, often held in high esteem. Their roles were often as caregivers, healers, or herbalists.

Many of the psychiatrists, psychologists, and students in the crowded auditorium had previously not given much thought to these notions of gender diversity. Instead anyone who expressed discomfort with their assigned gender might have been considered to be suffering from a disorder, one that might be cured with talk therapy. For a long time, medical and psychological professionals lacked education about gender diversity, making it difficult for transgender people to access appropriate care and services. At least this presentation sparked discussions about how to provide better, more inclusive medical and mental health services to lesbian, gay, bisexual, and transgender people.

According to the 1994 version of the *Diagnostic and Statistical Manual of Mental Disorders, DSM- IV,* the accepted reference for psychiatry and medicine at the time Jenni came out to us, Gender Identity Disorder (GID) was the diagnosis given to people who expressed a persistent discomfort with their assigned sex. This version was still in use when Jenni came out and when Dr. Coleman came to speak at Grand Rounds.

In 2013, due in part to greater understanding and awareness of transgender issues, the DSM-5 replaced *Gender Identity Disorder* with

Gender Dysphoria. In doing so, it removed the stigma often surrounding a disorder, and changed the focus to the dysphoria, or discomfort, experienced by a transgender person. Adults, adolescents and children diagnosed with Gender Dysphoria typically report a persistent inability to identify with their assigned gender. Without treatment, over time the sense of being in the wrong body can interfere with a person's ability to function in accordance with the expectations of society for the behavior of a male or a female.

Diagnosing a person with Gender Dysphoria offers the possibility of helping that person chose an appropriate course of treatment to alter the body, or supporting the person to be comfortable as neither male nor female, but somewhere in between. The involvement of a multidisciplinary team of physicians and psychologists insures that people who are transgender receive proper care and support if they embark on a course of action to change their bodies to match their identity. Gender confirmation surgery, previously known as sex reassignment surgery, is a big step, the ultimate goal for some, but not all who are transgender. Some may choose hormone treatments to change the body or surgery to alter it, while still others may just want the freedom to express their gender preferences with hairstyles, make-up, and clothing.

We have come a long way in understanding gender diversity. With increased exposure and media attention, society is becoming better educated and more aware. Attitudes have begun to change, but there is still more to be done to insure the safety of sexual minority children and adults in school, at home, and in society. No one should be afraid to express their gender identity or be forced out of their homes to live on the streets. In the years since Jenni came out to us, transgender people may have become more visible, but sadly, they are not always recognized as entitled to equal protection under the law. Even today there are those who seek to undermine, marginalize, criminalize, and discriminate against transgender people, even proposing laws to deny human rights and services, including health related services, to people who are gay, lesbian, or transgender.

This narrow-mindedness and prejudice has led to far too many hate crimes and far too many tragedies. Especially sad are the many young people for whom suicide seems the only alternative to escape harassment and bullying. While it may be somewhat easier to come out today because of increased media exposure of transgender children and adults, the potential for negative reactions or abuse by family, friends, and society still exists. Lack of acceptance and support by family can lead to depression and suicide, or to running away from home. Gender minority youth who seek refuge in big cities, hoping to find acceptance or at least anonymity, often find themselves among the homeless, living on the fringes of society, vulnerable to the darker forces of humanity, including prostitution and drug abuse. Without proper services for young people who are homeless, this is often the only way to survive, the only way to provide oneself with basic needs for food and shelter.

Our current vocabulary for discussing gender diversity has expanded beyond lesbian, gay, bi-sexual, transgender, inter-sexed, and questioning (LGBTIQ) to be even more inclusive with terms such as sexual minority or gender nonconforming. Nonetheless, compared to the general population, transgender and gender non-conforming youth are at far greater risk for attempting, or successfully committing, suicide. While there may be multiple reasons for a person to want to end their life, one thing remains clear. More must be done to insure the safety and well-being of transgender youth and adults. They too are entitled to the same basic human rights and legal protections as everyone else. The onus now is on society to recognize the richness and diversity in humanity, and for parents to raise children to be true to themselves and comfortable in their bodies, even if it means changing it to match their identity.

Chapter 20

Gender Dichotomy to Gender Fluidity

In mid 1990s, when Jenni came out, the availability of therapy and counseling to support a person through transition was limited and not always readily accessible. Fortunately for Jenni, support and resources for transgender youth and young adults were available in Portland, where she lived. Throughout the country, the diagnosis of Gender Identity Disorder implied to many in the medical, psychological, and lay communities the presence of an illness, a problem that begged for a cure. Despite the change in the professional diagnostic label in the DSM-5, there are still those who believe that a person who identifies as a member of the opposite sex, and wishes to live in a manner consistent with his or her identity, will abandon these thoughts with therapy. Some of these therapeutic methods might appear to be relatively benign, while others are downright coercive and abusive. Even with increased awareness and education, some transgender people are forced to undergo conversion therapies which attempt to change a person's sexual orientation or gender identity. While it is banned in some states, it is still practiced throughout most of the country.

Over the years I began to understand that previously held notions of gender identity no longer apply. The mismatch between biological sex and gender identity may be sensed in childhood, yet the decision to verbalize the discrepancy and take steps to live as one identifies may not occur until adolescence or adulthood. Without a framework for understanding gender differences, the sense that one is different, while being persistent, might not be understood, and questions about one's gender identity might be so difficult to verbalize that they are pushed away and denied.

This, as she revealed to us, is what it was like for Jenni. Unable to find information to answer his questions about why he felt that he was meant to be a girl, Joshua pushed those uncomfortable feelings away without revealing them to anyone. He tried to deny them until he could no longer conceal his identity as a woman. Jenni wanted to explore her options on her own, coming out to herself before coming out to anyone else.

Once Jenni was permitted to start a course of hormones to alter her body, her breasts began to develop, her hips began to widen, and her features softened. She endured many hours of electrolysis to destroy the roots of the thick facial and body hair that she felt had no business growing on her face. The hormones, however, did not have an effect on the vocal cords which had already developed to produce a characteristically male voice. Surgery to shave off the Adam's apple to minimize its typical male prominence would have been yet another step in the process towards eventual gender confirmation surgery.

In the context of what I learned about gender dysphoria, the idea that human development does always proceed in a neat predictable manner began to make sense to me. In the beginning, all embryos look pretty much the same. Based upon the pattern of the chromosomes, XX for female, XY for male, with rare anomalies that do not fit into the typical pattern, the genitalia begin to differentiate at around six or seven weeks after conception. Genetics and hormones exert their powerful influence transforming an undefined embryo to look more or less female or male, or anywhere in between.

Hormone surges, including testosterone and estrogen in balanced amounts at critical points in times, determine the course of development. These hormone surges continue to influence physical, mental, and emotional development throughout infancy and childhood, most notably at puberty and adolescence, and continuing throughout adulthood.

Typically, the female fetus develops to become a female child, and the male fetus develops as a male child, with matching hormone production and brain development. Since physical characteristics of gender and gender identity are independent of one another, many possibilities exist. An interruption or variation in the timing or amount of hormones might affect how the fetus develops, both physically and mentally. So much of life depends upon a delicate balance. The same combination of ingredients, put together in the same way, may result in different outcomes, as anyone who bakes cakes can tell you. Any number of variables, known or unknown, have the potential to profoundly affect the course of development, or in the case of baked goods, the finished product.

Infants born with ambiguous genitalia present a difficult challenge. In the past, surgical intervention might have been recommended to better define the sex of the child, or more exactly to categorize the baby as male or female. For example, an underdeveloped penis might be formed into a clitoris and a vagina, and the parents advised to raise the child as female – a female who would never menstruate, or be capable of reproducing. Gender identity, however, may not be known until expressed by the child when she or he becomes verbal. If such a child later identifies as male, consistent with his genetic blueprint, decisions made early in development might lead to serious internal conflict.

Gender identity, as distinguished from biological sex or perceived gender, is a very personal issue that does not fit neatly into two simple categories. There is plenty of room along the continuum from male to female for a person to identify, regardless of what their body or society dictates. Removing the constraints of binary or categorical thinking allows for free expression to identify as male, female, or neither male nor female, but somewhere in between.

Throughout the life span, at any given point in time a male may appear very masculine, very feminine, or anywhere in between. The same is true for females. An observer may perceive a person to be more or less female or male based on physical characteristics, hairstyle, clothing, social role, and behavior. Based on these observations, certain assumptions might be made, depending on the life experiences of the observer. Some social and occupational roles typically attract either males or females, however this too has begun to change, thanks to the bravery of those who dare to cross expected gender lines to pursue their dreams or express their true identity. Credit must be given to male nurses and teachers, female doctors and auto mechanics, to mention just a few examples of people who diverge from stereotypical expectations.

At any point in time, individuals may be attracted to members of the same sex, opposite sex, both sexes, or they may be asexual. Humans are a diverse lot in just about all aspects of life. Male, female, gay, straight, transgender, questioning, or anywhere in between does not matter at all. Only individuals themselves are in a position to define who they are, and whom they love.

When Jenni first came out, I was unclear on the distinction between gender identity and sexual orientation. It seemed incongruous that my child, a heterosexual male, could now be a lesbian woman. Jenni explained that she was always a woman, was always attracted to women, and therefore always a lesbian. It took a while for me to comprehend what she was saying. It was beyond anything that I had ever heard or given any thought, yet it began to make sense when she explained it to me.

Today there are parents who choose to wait until their children are able to express their identity before making life-changing decisions for them, especially in situations where the sex of a child at birth is ambiguous. When a child's body does not match his or her self-identity, awareness of the mismatch may come early. There are instances of children stating, as soon as they are verbal, that they are not a boy or not a girl, despite what their parents or their bodies tell them. This does not mean the child will ultimately seek to change gender, however, such strong assertions warrant further exploration. Once it is confirmed that the best course of action for such a child is to transition, a course of hormone treatment might be prescribed prior to puberty to facilitate development according to the child's identity.

Alternately, a person might identify as neither male nor female. Rather they might fit somewhere on the gender identity continuum, but not necessarily at either end, as defined in our culture. To take it a step further, the concept of gender fluidity is beginning to make its way into our consciousness, allowing a child to state his or her gender preference, or to help children and their families to be comfortable with ambiguity, neither male nor female, but somewhere in between.

This is not a new concept. Rather it is one that has been culturally suppressed through efforts to deny or forbid expressions of diversity in gender identification. Throughout the world, and throughout history, there are societies of indigenous people who acknowledge the fact that some people identify as members of the opposite sex, somewhere in between, or neither, and recognized as having a place and a role, sometimes a highly revered place. In some societies, they are marginalized and discriminated against. As we learn more about transgender people, and more transgender and gender non-conforming people tell their stories, the better we will be able to understand the richness and diversity of humanity.

Jenni's transition forced me to look outside the box, and sometimes remove the box, to get to a place where things are not always black or white, good or bad, important or insignificant, or male or female. I reflected on dichotomous thinking, and how it deprives us of appreciating the richness of all the variations in humanity. Jenni would be pleased to know this. Even as a child, Jenni kept us on our toes, as she would sometimes quip, challenging almost everything and forcing us to look at even the simplest things in a new light, a different light, from a perspective we did not know existed. It was a characteristic about my child that I always admired, even though there were times I found it frustrating and exhausting.

Telling Jenni's story helps keep her spirit alive, and gives me an opportunity to share what I have learned. The more people know and understand, the greater the chance transgender, lesbian and gay individuals and couples will feel safe to enjoy the same human rights as all other members of society. What little I have done to help that process along by sharing information and explaining what it means to be transgender protects me from my own unbearable sadness of losing my child.

At a family gathering in our home after Jenni died, I overheard a cousin trying to explain to his six year old son who Jenni was, and that Jenni used to be a boy named Joshua. I could see in this father's eyes when he saw me from across the room that he was begging to be rescued. Clearly, he was uncomfortable. Before I could step in, another cousin, a little girl only slightly older than the boy, heard the conversation and came to the rescue. She said that she too had a hard time understanding how Joshua could become a girl, but after a while, when she thought about it, she started to understand that some people just don't match their bodies, and they have to change their bodies. Hands on hips, she emphatically declared, So *now I understand!*

The little boy seemed satisfied with her explanation and both children went off to play. The father breathed a sigh of relief. He had no idea how to explain what he could not understand, and what made him uncomfortable. All I could think was that I have great hope for the next generation whose minds will be open to worlds of possibilities with greater awareness, sensitivity, and acceptance.

Karen Shiffman Lateiner

Chapter 21

Reaching Out

A few years after Jenni's death, an obituary in our local newspaper caught my attention. A young man, a college student, who grew up a block from our home, was found dead in his dormitory room. Not knowing the family, or the young man, I was reluctant to intrude, yet I felt compelled to reach out. The prohibitions I heard throughout my life played over and over in my head – *mind your own business, leave them alone, and don't bother them.* At the same time, I could not stop thinking about this young man's death and the family's loss.

Following my instinct, I telephoned the home. The boy's mother answered. I offered my condolences and told her I understood what she was going through. My words, meant to be supportive, offended her. She screamed that I did not understand, and could not possibly understand. Waiting for a break in her response, I told her I did understand, as I too lost my child and knew what it must be like for her. She was silent. Finally, she asked to meet. A few days later we met in my garden. Without a word, we opened our arms to each other and sobbed on each other's shoulder, sobbing for our mutual loss, sobbing to share the pain. Silently we communicated deep understanding, as we gave each other strength in knowing exactly what the other was experiencing. We knew.

As the weeks and months passed, we met for long walks together in the park. A step ahead of her in the grieving process, I understood what she was going through and served as a guide to what she might expect. We heard of another young man in our community who died and we both felt compelled to reach out. Tragically young people continued to die in our community, a situation that became all the more salient to our small group of grieving parents.

Every month our little group of grieving parents met, to console each other, share stories about our children, and imagine what they would be like if they could be with us. We wondered if they knew each other before they died, and what they would say if they saw their parents talking about them. Sometimes we found ourselves laughing at our stories, but when silence fell like a curtain over our conversations, we paused to wipe away tears we could not hold back. We guided the newcomers, shared their grief, and understood, really understood, what they were experiencing. Ultimately, it is a journey one must take alone, but support even if just a nod, a word, or any acknowledgment helps to make it somewhat more manageable.

At our meetings, we dealt with practical matters, such as getting through holidays, anniversaries, birthdays. There were no answers, no rules, only suggestions. The hardest question of them all was what to say when asked about the composition of our family. So many years later, it remains one of the most difficult challenges for me. Each time I must decide if telling the truth is worth diverting the conversation to a subject most find uncomfortable, or if I should welcome the opportunity to keep my child's spirit alive.

When people ask

What shall I say when people ask,
Do you have children?
What shall I say when people ask,
Is this child you proudly speak of your only one?

We had two. She is the surviving child.
To say otherwise, a lie.
One cannot deny a lifetime, no matter how short.
There was a past,
A history of experiences and relationships.

Meeting new people brings awkward moments.
Small talk made about the places we lived,
The people I have known.
And if a connection from the past emerges,
Shall I acknowledge if it is linked to my child?
The child who is dead.

Following the thread seems natural.
But then comes the inevitable question,
Where is he now?
With the inevitable answer,
No longer with us, it's been this many years.

Next the inevitable blanching of the person,
The clutching of the heart, the silence.
My immediate reaction.
I touch the person's shoulder and say,
I'm sorry – I did not mean to upset you.

The silence grows uncomfortable.
I tell them more about my child, or try to shift the focus.
Afterwards, I wonder why I uttered the truth.
Why tell when I have no desire to upset anyone.

Talking about one's children seems natural.
Living or dead - forever part of our lives.
Stories keep memories and spirits alive.
I cannot erase the fact my child is dead,
Nor can I erase an entire existence.
Death is a reality.
A reality I live with every day.

I am who I am because of the deaths I knew.
Worst of all, my child's death.
Sudden, needless, and far too soon.
It is my reality - I cannot deny it.
I am sorry if it makes anyone feel uncomfortable,
But it makes me uncomfortable to be asked.

And so, I remain cheerful, look to appreciate all I have.
All there is to celebrate about life.
When others tell me about their parents, or their children,
I listen attentively and encourage them to tell me more.

But deep inside, my heart aches for what
I will never know about my parents,
Or my child who is dead.
Instead, I wonder what it would be like if...

—KSL, 2005

Chapter 22

The Tree of Life and Death

Sometime before her death, I asked my mother to stay up late with me to share whatever she knew about our family history. Sadly, much of the history of Eastern European Jews who immigrated to America before and after the turn of the twentieth century was left behind in the old country by people, like my grandparents, anxious to start a new life.

On taped-together pieces of graph paper spread out on the dining room table, I penciled in the names, approximate dates of birth and death, and bits of anecdotal history my mother shared with me. My father's line was marked by cardio-vascular disease and premature deaths. The cause of his young mother's death when he was a child was unknown. One of his first cousins, a young woman, just twenty-one years old, died suddenly of a cerebral aneurysm or blood clot. No one is quite sure. My father's sister, a daring young woman who travelled halfway across the country to Texas in the sidecar of her husband's motorcycle, died of leukemia while still in her thirties. My father's brother succumbed to a massive stroke at the age of fifty-two. Two years later my own father, just fifty-five years old, had a fatal heart attack. My paternal grandfather's brother started a branch of the family in England. I later learned that quite a few of my father's first cousins who grew up in London also died prematurely, mostly in their fifties, also from cardio-vascular disease.

When Jenni started hormone treatment, I consulted my doctor to ask his opinion. He listened attentively, thought about it a few moments, and said that it might not be such a bad idea given the medical history of men in my father's line. We laughed. Ironically, estrogen, thought to protect against heart attack and stroke did nothing to protect Jenni from early death.

On another occasion, in search of information about the history of my family, I visited my father's aunt, my great-aunt Anna, the mother of the young woman who died suddenly in her twenties. My aunt told me that she cried bitterly when her older brother, my grandfather, left their village in Russia to bring his wife and child, her playmate, to America in the late 1890's. She wanted to go with them, but her parents felt that at four years old she was too young. When she was fourteen years old, her parents granted her wish and allowed her to travel alone by boat to New York. A few years later, her parents also left their home, but found it too difficult to adjust to life in America. They decided to go back home to Russia. Terribly homesick, my aunt decided to go back with them, but at the last minute she changed her mind to stay with her brother. When she waved good-bye, she never thought it would be the last time she would see them. World War I broke out and they were never heard from again. I learned much later that all the Jews remaining in their village were killed, just one of many horrific tragedies of the twentieth century – families separated and slaughtered at the hands of hateful, intolerant people with no regard for human life. Unbearable pain and suffering, yet we, as a species, go on.

I see the adventurous spirits of my great-aunt and her daughter in my daughter, Sarah, who at fourteen years old joined our English cousins on their family trip to Prague and later lived in Hungary for a year as a high school exchange student. As an adult she was unafraid to venture into an occupation traditionally held by men, thus helping to break down barriers for other women in the automotive industry as a role model in the industry.

My mother's line was apparently a bit sturdier than that of my father. The death from pneumonia of my mother's younger brother at the age of sixteen was an exception. I never knew this uncle, but heard countless stories of his creative mind and keen sense of humor. In keeping his spirit alive, my mother told us funny stories about his antics. He kept pigeons on the roof of their house, and just to get a laugh walked around on stilts with an alarm clock strapped around his wrist. It is not too hard to imagine the genetic roots of Jenni's personality as I remember some of his childhood antics.

My own experience of death began at a young age. By the time I was seven years old, two of my grandparents died. Up until my father's death when I was fifteen, it seemed to me that funerals and sitting *Shiva* was a frequent occurrence in my family. Most of these deaths were sudden. My maternal aunt's husband, the father of three young children, suffered a heart attack while on a family vacation at the beach. Then, my father's brother died, leaving his wife and two sons. Not long before my father died, my maternal grandmother came to live with us, displacing my sister and me from the bedroom we shared. She died a month later of leukemia. My mother barely had time to mourn the loss of her mother before she too became a widow, just three months later, leaving her alone to figure out how to manage as a single parent and sole breadwinner.

At fifteen, I was a child without a father or grandparents, with little support from an extended family adjusting to the altered composition of their own families. Most of my first cousins were already fatherless. Not long after, my maternal uncle's teenaged son was killed in an automobile accident during a family vacation. Less than ten years later their young adopted daughter died of a heart condition. My childhood, overshadowed by sadness and loss, was put on hold for so many periods of mourning.

A year after Jenni's death, a friend died of cancer, a year after that another died suddenly of a heart attack, and two years after that, yet another of cancer. Three very close, very dear friends, all in what should have been their best years, now senselessly dead. The bubble I had learned to construct for myself shielded me from overwhelming emotions. From this place of self-protection, I was able to help others deal with grief, assuring them that it is possible to go on living and maybe even laugh again. I had practice. Death was just another part of life.

On September 11, 2001, I watched the second tower of the World Trade Center collapse. I saw it as I rushed home from work to be with my family on the day we were certain the world as we knew it might be coming to an end. Twelve miles away in Montclair, it was clearly visible. Traffic stopped at an otherwise busy intersection, a place with a clear vantage point to the skyline of Manhattan. All eyes were on the horizon as everyone's radios were tuned to simultaneous reports of the horror we had just witnessed. Three thousand lives lost in the space of minutes. Three thousand grieving families! Three thousand stories to be told. It was unfathomable. Again, I went numb, crawled into my bubble, and continued on my way home as I listened to the stunned newscasters on the radio describe the scene. At home, we stood in front of the television watching the same scene over and over again.

I saw it. I watched it happen. Repeating the same thing over and over, aloud or to myself, always in a flat, emotionless voice, not believing it actually happened, turned it into a reality. I thought of all the disasters throughout the world, all the war, all the senseless destruction, and all the grieving families.

Coincidently, Sarah had flown home the night before from Arizona, where she was studying automotive technology after graduation from college. I shuttered at the thought that my child could have been on one of those planes or any other plane that had gone down by accident or an act of terrorism. Manhattan was closed down for days as silence fell on this city that was once alive and vibrant. The three of us held each other tight, horrified and helpless, reminding us yet again of how fragile life is. I could relate to the personal losses, to each one individually, but the enormity of it all, so close to home, was overwhelming. I could barely breathe.

Throughout the ages, people left families, villages, and countries to seek better lives, and to escape from hate and violence. Some never saw their families again. I reflected on the burdens of mothers and fathers, and on the human condition. We are born and grow under our parents' guidance and nurturance. We bind ourselves to another human being, create a circle of friends, usher in new lives, and nurture the next generation. Along the way death intervenes, taking mothers, fathers, friends, and children. In the normal course of events, life ends after fulfilling the mission of giving life and watching that life grow and mature. Children should not die before their parents. Yet they do, and somehow we find the strength to go on, finding comfort in knowing it is possible to go on.

When I was young, I wondered why my mother and grandmother sometimes stopped what they were doing to let out a sigh, a deep long sigh. I understand it now as a sign of self-preservation. It is what we do to stay alive. Just as generations of mothers before me, I too sometimes stop what I am doing to let out a sigh, a deep long sigh, just as they did.

The Meaning of a Sigh

Breathe in. Close eyes.
Hold. Hold some more.
Hold as memories flash by.
Memories too painful to describe.
Memories masked by the present.
Emotions too intense to contain.

Good times. Bad times. Times of laughter.
Times of tears. Unspeakable terror.
Memories of loss. Death. Annihilation.
Parents, children, siblings, entire families
Torn apart by death, disease, hate, war.
The list goes on.
Impossible to ponder, and still breathe.

Expel the long held breath,
Release with a resounding hum.
Hmmmmmmmmmm.
Breathe in. Breathe out.
The relentless expression of life.
Intrusions expelled in a long, deep sigh.
A pause to reflect. Breath returns.
Life goes on.

—KSL, 2013

Chapter 23

Memes and an After-Life Legacy

Meme: An idea, behavior, or style that spreads from person to person within a culture. —Wikipedia

Joshua left his persona behind to move on to a new life, a new beginning, as the person she was meant to be. Even her résumé left no clues that her professional experience was acquired as Joshua S. Lateiner. Instead Jenni marketed her skills as a computer programmer and software developer, leaving her past a continent away. Her former employers in Oregon spoke very highly of her when we met them after she died. They had been well aware of the fact that she was in the process of transitioning from male to female. Even at that time, her boss and fellow employees made whatever accommodations were necessary for her to feel comfortable during what might have been a terribly awkward and potentially dangerous time for anyone in the process of changing their gender. By the time Jenni was hired by Netscape in California, she presented well as a woman, and as far as we knew, her gender was not questioned. If it had been, it apparently did not matter in that environment. They were more interested in her brilliant mind.

When we met some of her Netscape co-workers after her death, the subject of gender never came up. Again, our conversation centered on Jenni's charm and accomplishments. We were presented with a box of software, still in its original shrink wrap. *The Java Developers Kit* was the product of Jenni's team, containing code written mostly by her. This represented but a small part of her legacy.

Joshua had written about memes before Facebook, before Twitter, even before the concept of a meme made its way into the general vocabulary. He talked about a mind-machine interface, imagining thoughts and ideas transferred from one person to another via an implanted chip. With each new technological advance, I stop to wonder - if only Jenni were alive today. If only she could experience the future she imagined and played a small role in creating. What a loss for us, and the world.

Today we talk about an idea becoming a meme as it travels through time and space, mostly through the Internet, until everyone understands its meaning. Maybe that is the meaning of spirit. Maybe a person's spirit lives on as a meme. Maybe the transmission of that meme, the meme that is a person's spirit, is the afterlife. I began to construct my own views of the universe, the meaning of life, and the meaning of afterlife, comforted by the thought of Jenni's spirit as a meme I can share with others.

As Jenni looked to the future, she remained grounded in the present with an understanding of life beyond her years. On the monument we erected at the cemetery in New Jersey, where her ashes are buried is inscribed Jenni's sentiment and philosophy that she shared with us before she died.

Don't forget the simple things. The magical moments
When you get a moment of peace to breathe in and
Reflect on all there is to celebrate about life.
I strongly believe that feeling is it. If you can
Reach that peace you know all you need to know
In terms of uncovering happiness and living a
great life.

—Jenni, 1998

I recite those words often. When we visit the cemetery, I stop to read, remember, and reflect. Once when Roger and I were visiting Jenni's grave, the director of the cemetery stopped his car when he spotted us. He said he often paused to read the inscribed message and hoped one day to meet someone who could tell him more about this wise young person. We told him about our child and left grateful that Jenni's spirit continues to live on. The past cannot be changed, but I can keep the memory of my child alive, and celebrate all there is to celebrate about life as the future unfolds.

Jenni's fiancée, Margaret, posted on her website a piece Jenni wrote May 30, 1998, just a few days before she died, along with a brief note about Jenni:

If you asked me this morning what information I'd like you to have, I'd say the following: Try to imagine self-aggregating structures of information...a community, website/project, a civilization, a culture. Now imagine the culture going about the hard work of describing itself as itself. Speaking in myths, at first, and then discovering empirical science. As we begin the quest of knowing about ourselves more completely, we can ask "What can I do to improve the community in which I willingly participate?"

One participates in a community only by choice, one desires either:

Death: Pleasure from the self

Life: Pleasure from others (received in a way which loosely correlates to the pleasure which you bring others, but there is much randomness: Imagine, "I'll give you a dollar. You give me whatever you like! I'll take nothing, perhaps you'll just ask me for another dollar, or maybe I will receive millions!")

The brave person seeks pleasure from others. As anyone who knows the difference between masturbation and sex can tell you - sex is definitely different depending on the number of intentional systems participating. Even if one pretends they are the second person, touching themselves, they're a closed system - they know their own actions despite any attempt to feign innocence (e.g., if one imagined they were two people, one person making love to another...)

Thus, the greatest pleasure comes when we expose ourselves to unknowns (my taste of course). If one prefers masturbation, and seeks to give nothing to fellow people, feel free to withdraw from society. Understand then that the common culture does not apply to you.

The common culture optimizes itself by seeking to teach happiness to itself. Thus the common culture only wishes to a certain extent to pleasure itself - which would be true if it did not know of anything other than itself.

As a community learns of others, it wishes to share and exchange knowledge so that all may grow in happiness *over time. Life is a process of finding ways to make more people happier over greater periods of time. Any other goals are superficial and not to be trusted.*

So if someone asks you to help them build a nuclear weapon, ask yourself how this will increase the general happiness quotient. Will this make you happier? Will it make your community happier? Will your children's children's lives be happier because of this action? What if one has no children, would I intentionally do something which has the power to hurt others? Do I not feel the pain of the lives whose happiness will be squelched? If I do not feel the pain of those who will be hurt by my actions, is there some righteous part of me that would seek to destroy myself if I were self-aware enough to understand how much I hurt myself by seeking to destroy others?

Free yourself from the tyranny of the incomplete happiness that one earns with ill-considered actions. It is a crime to consider too small of a moment when attempting to determine the outcome of a situation. We should feel a moral compulsion to accumulate accurate knowledge into aggregates that are useful! Furthermore, we should feel a compulsion to use this structured information to the best of our abilities. To fail to build efficient information structures to assist in enlightened decision making is the ultimate crime, for one cheats oneself and one's society from the happiness which further knowledge might bring.

[Editor's note: Yes, the above paragraph provides a moral and ethical justification for my job as a Java developer building decision-support web-applications :-)]

A community and a culture must satisfy the basic needs of any individual: to embark on any project! To feel as though any goal worthy of attempting might be attainable by anyone with the desire to seek that goal! To feel as though all people are capable of messianic caliber judgments, and that all people would make that same decision if they had the same information. To feel that all of us try to work together towards the mutual goals of increasing the likelihood that everyone in the community will have a moment that evening in which they think to themselves, "Life is good: I am healthy, and I have sufficient human contact to sustain myself. From my fellow humans, I receive infinity of riches: shelter, food, companionship, empathy. I shall never be in need as long as I have human companionship."

I need never fear. I know myself and my universe and welcome learning more about myself and my environment. It has all been said before — but when we start living by the basic precepts of harmony and happiness. Peace and Liberty. Freedom and Justice. Deep resonances of educated thought and communal wisdom impart our lives with richness.

*It is my hope that other people who have reached epiphany in their lives will seek to share it with others. It is my hope that I and others will try to remember **to think**, to be aware of as large a moment as possible when considering what the next action should be. Recognize the limits of the mind - create habits of thought to speed your decisions, but know the limits of your own habits so that you will remain forever unbounded.*

Be capable of re-deducing yourself from scratch at any given moment. When you ever need to deal with a subject in its entirety, you will need to bring to the discussion a thorough knowledge of yourself in order for your thoughts to be of real value. After all, your thoughts are a product of yourself, and what it is that you are becomes reflected in your contributions.

Create yourself, know yourself. Build yourself into the person you wish to be, and realize that with every action you are joining into the communal dance, even if you are the only one to perceive your action. Respect yourself -- you should understand your own ability to influence yourself!

Is it possible that something as simple as taking a moment out of a busy day to smile and reflect on the moment can make the world a better place?

*People complain that there is never time for any of the great projects. Eternity is made up of a large number of Mondays, Tuesdays, Wednesdays, Thursdays, Fridays, Saturdays and Sundays. Historic events typically happen on days that bear one of those seven names. Every moment, every***thing*** existent is holy in some small way.*

Is today the day you would make the decision to bring into reality some vision that would profoundly impact the happiness of thousands? Or is today simply the day to take out the recycling?

When the hour of celebration arrives, have you brought anything to the community, or do you just drink the wine of others?

Do you seek to learn and improve on the party-tricks of previous generations? Or do you blindly serve bleach instead of beer thinking that those who came before you didn't know what they were doing?

Question your own questioning of the past — and recognize the irony of the angst-ridden Gen-X'er denouncing tradition while drinking a beer...the formula for brewing grain into an enjoyable alcoholic elixir being a centuries-old tradition.

Respect the moment. Life is holy - we are all part of creation. You might perceive me as an atheist or a polytheist, or one who perceived that everything is part of the divine - that existence is a blessing and that the human being is such a cool thing because it can turn dreams into realities, giving voice to ghosts that can live longer than a single lifetime. For generations, people have dreamed of space travel, and it happened. Be careful what you wish for - we are all powerful, and we might find that we can create the experience we asked for

Me? I want to share the happiness of life with others. I have transcended intolerance (even my own self-intolerance) and learned to understand the unique gifts that all existent things bring. I have learned to accept and even cherish my own mortality. I have a chance in life to learn, and attempt to expand the happiness-giving communal knowledge and share anything new I learn with others, that the new information might lead to more happiness in the future.

Whether or not I live forever through genetically related children, I will have left my mark through a billion daily interactions. I hope their sum total swayed in the direction of increasing the happiness of the human experience. I think it would improve my own experience if we all agreed to try to increase the happiness of experience.

When I speak of happiness, perhaps I mean strength and satisfaction. The feeling of awe one gets when something cool happens - especially something that one has worked with others to achieve. For example, when fireworks get set off - what a great achievement! Such knowledge had to be employed, such skills - to produce the spectacle!

If I had to explain the universe, I'd say that it is the way in which energy sings to itself. The tune is ever changing, because the state-space of all possible song is so vast, thus the state of the universe unfolds.

The idea the energy would coalesce into matter and bring forth humans capable of remarking on this — many of the most probable things eventually happen. The universe isn't going to run out of time. Even if our physical universe collapses, there will be others.

Which means basically that, in theory, you can do whatever the hell you want and then die. That's pretty easy. However, if you put your mind to it, you can have a lot of fun! Especially if you collaborate with others.

What would I ask of creation? Share the love! Bring something creative to the next party...Teach me something that will make me smile, and be there for me when I need compassion. Help me reflect during my times of decision. Be a whole person unto yourself and help teach me the same joy that comes from being a whole, growing person (an unbounded system, constantly evolving.)

If we all did this - if we all saw our fellow self-aware beings as essentially themselves with a different set of circumstances - then we'd be all set.

If we ever evolve to the point where we can reason with an alien intelligence without bringing out the worst parts of human nature, then it will be as if the messiah arrived. I suggest granting a "presumed sentient until proven otherwise" to any energy system that seeks an audience.

Thus I would recommend that any pattern of energy (human or otherwise) be presumed to be a rational self-aware system until proven otherwise

Corporations should hire people as full time visionaries to observe the business and help insure that people's experience with the company are positive.

Why do I pontificate thusly? I have seen, because I have dared to look where others shield their eyes. I can perceive senseless pain and suffering as well as priceless beauty - open yourself to it all and attempt to learn the rhythm of existence so that I may dance in celebration.

—Jennifer Lateiner, copyright May 30, 1998

Biography:

Jennifer Lateiner was a 24-year-old born in New York City. She attended myriad life celebrations with the like-minded San Francisco Bay residents. She claimed to have found an inner understanding of herself and the universe that brought her great joy, or at least that is what she said the last time I saw her buying a used velvet dress, smoking clove cigarettes along Telegraph in Berkeley.

—Margaret, 1999

* * * * *

182

Jenni's life-long friend, Erik Bloom, wrote a eulogy in her honor:

In writing today in honor of Jenni's memory, I am immediately faced with pronoun trouble. For myself, neither he nor she will do, since it is a total life I wish to do some small justice to, and revisionism only supplants one incomplete vision for another. But, the limits of language force me to make a choice, and awkwardness will not do. Jenni demonstrated and lived out the fact that each of us are, in truth, many people. A commonplace to be sure, unless pushed past comfortable limits and Jenni loved to push us all past comfortable limits. So out of respect for what Emily Dickinson called, "My second rank," as she added, "too small the first," who spoke, baptized and renamed herself as a self-conscious, mature adult, an adult, "Adequate and erect, with will to choose, or to reject," I will use 'she' throughout this essay. For the point is we are all more than we may appear to any one person, including oneself. Yet, the miracle of personality is that a marvelous consistency of character runs through all that we do, despite the surface contradictions. So, although each of us experienced his or her own Jenni, we all loved, fought, played with the same miracle that she was and is in the living imagination of our memory.

It's hard to remember, or at least think about, Jenni before she had a computer. The first to my memory was a Commodore 64, a simple creamy grey box which to me just looked like a fat keyboard — magic we took for granted. I remember watching her whacking away at the thing, each click of the keys making a small, hollow bang. I never was as interested in the string of symbols that ran across the screen until years later. But Jenni seemed to see the possibility of worlds there, worlds within worlds. For some reason, before then I have images of grand space flights in spaceships equipped with almost mythic abilities - mere faster-than-light speeds were not enough. I guess that's because children simply know that the unencumbered imagination accepts no limits other than its infinitely plastic fancy. Every child largely lives in their own fantasies, but Jenni seemed hell-bent on dragging them kicking and screaming into adulthood. We all return to those worlds of elastic facts where one might get off a desert island on which you've been stranded by making friends with a pig, snake, and an elephant, but usually only at night in our dreams.

Jenni preferred the day, or rather being awake, or better yet dreaming while awake. Marcel Proust wrote something to the effect that if dreaming a little was the problem then the solution was not to dream less, but to dream more, dream all the time. I never got a chance to share that one with Jenni, but I think she would have approved. One might say that Jenni was a dream on No-Doz (an often bad) pun on speed. One of my favorite talents of hers was her ability to let go a waterfall of weird nonsense, usually funny as hell, syntactically correct with Lewis Carroll-like logic. Jargon, slang, and high sounding philosophy tumbled over each other with the absurd grace of dancing clowns. Once, as she was doing the dishes, I heard her go on this way, improvised of course, for almost five minutes, taking breaths only every sixtieth word. I wish I could describe her beautifully silly laugh, the mouth pulled back in a gorgeous grin; the sound literally tickled, and sometimes actual tickling did follow. It physically hurts to think I will never hear it again. Some Catholic saint, I don't know which one, but certainly one of the less morbid ones, said that Paradise will be a gorgeous hilarity. I can't say I believe that that is where Jenni is now, but I know that is where Jenni was many times in her life, and where she took many others, including myself on numerous occasions. I often did not let it show that she did this for me, being the sour pus straight man that I am. This is why I wanted to tell you this today, which I never did get to tell Jenni herself.

I couldn't directly share in many of Jenni's dreams. To oversimplify, I preferred the past and Jenni the future. On long car trips, we'd always sing along to Simon and Garfunkel songs because we both knew the lyrics. We also liked the idea that it would make our parents proud – nostalgia, tradition, and all that funny stuff. Our differences were momentarily healed as we crooned "the words of the prophets are written on the subway halls and tenement halls..." For the longest time I was convinced, for some reason, that the line sang "bathroom stalls" instead of "tenement halls." Jenni though my version was better, I mean isn't a public bathroom where people publish their anonymous loves, prophecies, and truths, the stuff most of us won't say when others are around. Maybe it's just guys. Jenni, as a Tiresias of public bathroom experience, would know. Either way, Jenni herself was never anonymous. She loved to expand upon precisely what others would shrink away from. True it may have verged on what you might call Center of Attention Disorder, but then again she was definitely something to see long before her hair became acquainted with every color of the Manic Panic spectrum.

I am sure by now many have spoken of the sense that Jenni knew her time was to be limited and therefore squeezed in as much life as she could. I certainly remember Jenni telling me that she thought she was old by the time she was twenty two. But, I also remember her telling me that there was so much to do, so much to learn, build, explore, stumble on, trip over, leap over, and see that no amount of time was conceivably enough. So when I think back on a time when Jenni's refrigerator was filled with more vitamin bottles than food, I just don't get the sense of someone who wanted to live forever. I feel she intuited, despite her talk of immortality, that the true purpose of health was not to live longer, but to live more. We all remember the tape of Jenni when she was no more than five years old, already talking about the need to defeat death – an insult to her intelligence, as she would later have it.

I always imagined I would get to argue and laugh with Jenni about this stuff when we were both old. It never occurred to me that she might not be there. If anything I was ready to doubt whether I would make it. In the midst of one of my many depressive swoons, I confided this self-induced despair to Jenni. We were on the phone. I was in Storrs, Connecticut. She was in Portland, Oregon. In response she sounded on the edge of tears. I imagined they were there on her face. I realized then, or at least imagine I did, that even if everyone and everything I loved would be gone in the Brave New World that breathed a bleak future down my neck, Jenni would be there, very happy to see me. She would be there with her manic arms poised in the air ready to throw them around me. I could feel her tickle the grim look right off my face. I would be happy to grumble at her latest pun. I would be quietly thrilled to roll my eyes at her latest schemes, as she'd flaunt a new pair of anti-gravity boots, her old body doing flips like a cartwheeling child just to make me smile.

I struggle to know what else to say. I know, however, that it is not the past or the future that any of us have. It is only the fleeting moment that we live in, which runs faster away from us the more we try to grasp it. Even if we were to live forever, it is only there that we can exist. I believe, or rather at times, I have intuitively experienced, that there is an identity of all present moments though time, so that in clearly remembering and reimagining moments in the past, we intimate that they are just as real now as they were then. We can in a literal sense resurrect a piece of those who are physically gone, and have a sense of immortality of the deepest part of who they are and will be forever. So today, here with you, the immortal part of Jenni lives clothed again in the glory of our memories. I believe Jenni would have those memories be a parade of peacocks, as bright and flamboyant as hell. I apologize for not dressing the part. I did however, bring one drab hat. Schopenhauer wrote, "Our consciousness is as it were a lightning flash momentarily illuminating the night." I now tip my hat to the lightening flash that was Jenni and Joshua Lateiner, a flash who was exceptionally brilliant, the more so because she was brief.

Karen Shiffman Lateiner

Appendix 1

The Mimetic Web

While developing his company and promoting his software, Joshua gave numerous presentations to groups of doctors and hospital administrators in an effort to promote his software. He co-authored an article on three-dimensional imaging using his software as a diagnostic tool. *Stereoscopically guided characterization of three-dimensional dynamic MR images of the breast* by T Z Wong, J S Lateiner, T G Mahon, C S Zuo, and B L Buff appeared in the January 1996 of Radiology Society of North America Journal (Vol. 198, Issue 1).

That same year, he was invited to present a paper at the internationally renowned Ars Electronica Festival, but was unable to attend. Nonetheless, his paper was included in the 1996 Ars Electronica Festival Catalog. It is preprinted below with permission.

The Memetic Web
Joshua S. Lateiner

Memetics is a tool that may help explain certain complex phenomena relating to the interaction of material systems and intangible information. There is much to be explained, and memetics has only quite recently been proposed as a method for examining the world. Therefore, it may be wise to avoid applying memetic analysis to the evolution of complex socio-political power structures -

sidestepping the entire issue of advanced memetic analysis of truly complex issues until we have a firmer grasp of what memetics offers.

Postponing more complex analysis of memetic effects, what follows is a discussion of the evolutionary interplay of the physical, genetic and memetic realms. The Web is examined from the perspective of a memetically catalytic medium that accelerates both the transmission of memes and the realization of memetic artifacts.

3D: The Evolution of Memetic Evolution

A good introduction to memetic theory can be had by examining works by the 3D's - Darwin, Dawkins and Dennett. Darwin first formulated a method for arriving at the current level of complexity found in the biosphere via a process of natural selection in 1859 (Darwin, 1859). Dawkins first proposed that memes were new replicators - not self-replicating, per se, a type of "Virus of the Mind" (Dawkins, 1976). Dennett extended Dawkins' idea of memetic evolution when he proposed the concept of a "Universal Design Space" (Dennett, 1995, p. 143) in which natural selection is used as a catalytic tool to accelerate the exploration of "all things possible" in both the genetic and memetic realm.

The Universe To-Date

By extrapolating Dennett's proposal to include the physical realm, it may be possible to look at the unfolding of the known universe through evolutionary eyes. Perhaps the story would look something like the

II

following, in which we see matter "preferring" to organize into stable structures, followed by the emergence of replicating systems:

A uniform distribution of energy emerging from a point source expanded and cooled. Minor fluctuations in the continuity had non-linear repercussions as energy coagulated into matter. This material fell into countless arrangements as the universe unfolded, the more stable ones persisted and grew - galaxies emerged.

On a small planet on the outer rim of one of these galaxies, elemental materials churned in a primitive atmosphere. The elemental materials on this planet fell into countless arrangements, the more stable ones persisted and grew - life emerged.

Replicating arrangements of matter competed with each other for the resources required to grow/reproduce. The replicators that managed to survive gave birth to a new generation of similar replicators, some better suited than others to grow/reproduce in the current environment. We recognize this behavior as evolution.

The material tools that evolved to further replication of matter include DNA, the lingua franca of genetic evolution. One of the products of this (genetic) evolution included beings capable of communicating information. This made it possible to augment one's innate behavior on the fly, in response to information communicated. DNA served as a catalyst to speed up the process of finding designs for creating efficient replicators.

The story becomes more complex as new variables are introduced; viability is no longer based solely on the simple interaction between a genetic replicator and an impartial environment. Not only had other replicators become part of the environment, but the interaction of the replicators had evolved to the point where something as intangible as information could have a direct bearing on viability.

If two primitive beings are born with nearly identical genes into similar environments, we expect their phenotypes (the physical manifestation of one's genotype) and their ability to successfully grow/reproduce to be similar. This expectation can be explained using a strictly physical analysis of the situation. However, if one of these nearly-identical beings obtains information from another being regarding the creation of a fire, then suddenly their ability to successfully grow and reproduce is changed in response to a non-material factor. Intangible information now plays a role in differentiating between two replicating beings who would otherwise be (effectively) equivalently viable.

The non-material tools that evolved to further the process of replication are called "memes" - Richard Dawkins' term for a unit of thought. Memes produced by one replicator could be communicated to others via language. Cultures emerged, wherein a group of replicators benefitted from a set of shared memes. Memetic evolution is the process by which groups of memes are communicated and improved upon by a group of replicators - the memes that help to create an environment well suited to the further reproduction of memes (which likely implies an environment well suited to the further reproduction of genes) are the ones that persisted.

One species discovered that the memetic potency could be enhanced by creating a physical record. Complex human cultures emerged as memes evolved more rapidly with the assistance of written records. Writing served as a catalyst to speed up the process of finding designs for creating efficient cultures.

Thus we see that the rate of movement through Dennett's unified design space accelerated as catalytic agents (genes, memes, new memetic media - e.g. writing) emerged. Dennett extends Dawkins' suggestion that memetic evolution is similar to genetic evolution by proposing that it is all part of the same evolutionary process.

Catalytic New Media

Memes reproduce and evolve as ideas are communicated among memetic hosts. It is commonly accepted that human beings are good memetic hosts, capable of understanding, synthesizing and re-communicating memes; this is to be distinguished from memetic media, which serve to carry memes from one host to the next.

As new media for memetic transmission have come into use, they often catalyzed the rapid growth and evolution of the existing memes. The printing press improved upon hand-reproduced documents, making it possible to inexpensively transmit memes to a wider range of hosts. This helped accelerate cultural trends of the time. Furthermore, the introduction of the printing press also transformed the cultural environment to such an extent that new memetic structures arose from drastic mutations of the existing memes.

The 20th century has witnessed the introduction of several important mass media which are still in the process of being integrated into existing society. Radio and television provide a predominantly non-interactive means of communicating with a vast audience, while the Web provides a highly interactive means of allowing memetic hosts to acquire new memes (commonly called "surfing," as in "surfing the Web").

The Web differs from prior mass media in that it provides a more efficient method for communicating memes directly to hosts that are particularly susceptible to infection by a given meme. This efficiency is a result of the Web paradigm: memetic hosts directly seek new memes that appeal to them. While this behavior is not unique to Web surfing - for example, one often looks for books that are of particular interest - the Web accelerates and amplifies this behavior due to its highly interactive nature.

Is there a fundamental difference between the processes of selection, growth and reproduction of memetic technologies like the Web and traditional Darwinian evolution, or even the simple unfolding of the state of a complex physical system like a universe? Dennett would likely agree with the assertion that there is no fundamental difference, though memetic evolution occurs at a far faster rate than the plodding pace of genetics.

Conclusion: The Selfish Meme

There may indeed be a fundamental difference between the process of genetic and memetic evolution. Human memetic hosts are capable of intentional, conscious action - a factor that has far greater impact on the memetic evolutionary process than on the genetic process.

The intentionality of human memetic hosts makes it more likely that a human will re-transmit some memes much more widely than other, less interesting memes. The memetic host's desires are also shaped by memes, and it is this recursion of memetic influence that can create highly non-linear memetic effects like cultural fixation. This phenomenon may accelerate memetic evolution faster than expected.

This process is not without its physical effects - with the help of self-aware hosts (human beings), memes propagate and "wish" to be realized. Selfish memes are like a recipe for a delicious cake; the meme for making the cake embeds itself in one's mind and can motivate action (e.g. the baking of a cake). If a memetic impulse is acted upon, the meme artifact (the cake) may help further propagate the original meme (the idea that baking delicious cakes is desirable) when other memetic hosts are exposed to the artifact.

Selfish memes desire "realization" - the process of causing a memetic host to carry out some action. Successful selfish memes often cause memetic hosts to realize actions that assist in the transmission of the memetic content.

The process by which Americans became fascinated with futurism, space exploration, and the idea of landing a man on the moon could be described in terms of a system of selfish memes that established a self-reinforcing pattern that led to realization of the memetic concept (landing a man on the moon).

While a moon-landing may have eventually happened at some point in human history, its occurrence earlier in this century - perhaps much earlier than might have otherwise been expected - may be attributable to memetic feedback cycles.

The creation and continuing evolution of the Web may also be the result of a strong positively re-inforcing memetic feedback system. In 1984, Gibson's seminal novel "Neuromancer" was published - a near-future heavily inspired by current trends.

In it, he describes a cyberspace matrix: "Cyberspace. A consensual hallucination experienced daily by billions of legitimate operators, in every nation, by children being taught mathematical concepts ... A graphic representation of data abstracted from the banks of every computer in the human system. Unthinkable complexity." (Gibson, 1984, p. 51)

Gibson's novel, influenced by contemporary cultural trends, inspired programmers to work towards the systems they were already working towards - if they had not already been working towards such systems, Gibson might not have picked up on the themes that dominate "Neuromancer". Thus Gibson's novel helped accelerate a process that was already underway - a process which, among other developments, has helped to shape our vision of online information systems.

Acting as a memetic catalyst, the Web medium promotes the creation of memetic feedback cycles more than other media due to its interactivity and immediacy. The Web efficiently transmits memes that can have the effect of heightening desires in a way that causes a host to seek out and re-transmit related memes.

The Web is particularly kind to selfish memes that seek realization beyond simple retransmission by enabling people to work together towards the creation of more complex memetic artifacts. For example, memes that inspire citizens of a town to build a bridge across a river will be assisted by the Web's ability to augment human endeavors - helping the townspeople co-ordinate the resources necessary to actually build the bridge.

The Web will likely serve to accelerate memetic evolution, but the usefulness of memetics transcends the Web. Feedback cycles, the interplay of art and science, and large scale social movements also lend themselves to memetic analysis. Along a similar vein, the greatly accelerated memetic evolution evident on the Web will have effects that transcend memetics as selfish memes seek realization in the creation of memetic artifacts.

Certain memes have embedded themselves in our common culture, selfishly wishing to be realized: many in our society are fascinated by the memes like world peace and using technology to literally or figuratively transcend the body (Lateiner, 1992). It is likely that the Web will continue to play an increasing role in fueling our imagination and assisting in memetic realization.

NOTES:

Darwin, Charles (1859), On the Origin of Species by Means of Natural Selection, *London: Murray*

Dawkins, Richard (1976), The Selfish Gene, *Oxford: Oxford University Press*

Dennet, Daniel C. (1995), Darwin's Dangerous Idea, *New York: Simon and Schuster*

Gibson, William (1984), Neuromancer, *New York: Ace Books*

Lateiner, Joshua (1992), "Of Man, Mind and Machine: Meme-Based Models of Mind and the Possibility for Consciousness in Alternate Media," *in Dataspace: http://www.dataspace.com/documents/consciousness.html*

Acknowledgements

This book would not have been possible without the encouragement of friends and family, many of whom were relentless in urging me to publish my story. Surely they tired of asking, for nearly ten years since I started on this project, how my book was coming along, yet they remained patient, understanding the potential difficulty of writing such a memoir. Their inquiries kept me going, even as I wallowed in procrastination and self-doubt. Writing a book is difficult, yet when I gave myself the gift of time to focus on the process, it was satisfying to recall memories. Without a doubt, there were times when those memories brought tears, but more often I rejoiced at having had the privilege of being Jenni's mother and learning much about life from her. Her spirit, as well as the spirits of my ancestors, were with me every step of the way.

This book is dedicated to my family and friends whose love and support continue to be my lifeline, but especially to my husband, Roger, for his love and presence as we made our way through all the challenges we encountered throughout our lives together, including producing my memoir, and to my daughter, Sarah, for her love, friendship, and leadership. Most of all, this book is dedicated to Jenni, whom we knew for so many years as our son, Joshua, and to all those brave people with the courage to be true to themselves.

Throughout the journey described in this memoir, I have met many people who helped me understand transgender issues, especially Mary Boenke, Karen and Bob Gross, parent advocates, allies, and the many transgender people who kindly shared their stories. Over the years I have participated in writing seminars, conferences, and numerous writing workshops, even facilitating some of my own. Throughout all of these experiences, I discovered the powerful support of a community of writers, both aspiring and established. Their encouragement and guidance was invaluable, but best of all, I made lifelong friends along the way. It is with tremendous gratitude that I acknowledge the many teachers and numerous mentors who taught me to let my pen flow freely, in narrative or verse, members of various critique groups who read excerpts of my book and took the time to offer suggestions, some of which I actually used, and to my friends and family who encouraged me to tell my story. I am grateful to all of them for their insights and encouragement, especially Dr. Elizabeth McNeil and members of her writing workshop, which I attended though Arizona State University, for their thoughtful critiques and suggestions.

Again, I thank my husband Roger for reading and editing a very early draft, filling in missing information, and reading it again together with me as my manuscript progressed to its completion. It was difficult, at best, for him to relive the years about which I wrote. Old friends, Nancy Burke and Lorraine McConnell, shared their expertise as writers and editors, and new friends, Jacklyn Anderson and Tamara Santley, both of whom I met after I finished my manuscript, read my story through an objective lens to give me valuable feedback. I am especially grateful to Dr. Eli Coleman, Diane and Charles Gottlieb, and Gary Paul Wright for taking time to read my manuscript before publication. Their endorsements mean a lot to me. Randy Zucker helped with the cover design. I am most grateful to my book's shepherd Ann Videan, Videan Unlimited, LLC, for her expertise and patience as she worked with me to bring *Timeless Dance* to publication.

Jenni's fiancé, Margaret Oliver, shared her photographs of Jenni with us and granted permission to use the photograph she took of Jenni a few days before the accident for the cover of this book. An enlargement she made of the same photo remains a prized possession in our home. I am extremely grateful to remain in contact with her as she will always be a part of our family. Kara Kytle, Jenni's girlfriend friend from Boston and throughout her transition in Portland, also remained a close family friend and helped fill in historical details. Many thanks to Erik Bloom for allowing me to include the beautiful eulogy he wrote for his life-long friend.

A portion of the profits from the sale of this book will be donated to the Jenni-Josh Lateiner Memorial Fund. This fund was created with the help of generous donations made in memory of our child. The purpose of the Jenni Josh Lateiner Memorial Fund is to provide support to programs that provide education and resources concerning issues facing transgender and sexual minority youth and programs that prevent bullying. The fund logo, designed by Mor Erlich, an advocate for transgender youth and now a close family friend, is based on the photograph of Jenni dancing on the beach.

About the Author

Photo by Sarah Lateiner

Karen Shiffman Lateiner holds both an M.A. and M.Ed. in Educational Psychology. Throughout her personal life, and her professional career as an infant development specialist and mental health clinician, she has advocated safe and nurturing school environments for all children. Among her greatest influences are her two children who taught her much about life. After retirement, she and her husband traveled the country by motorhome before making Arizona their home. Combining her love of writing and the Sonoran desert, Ms. Lateiner encourages other writers in a *Hike and Write* group she created.